Kotlin Standard Library Cookbook

Master the powerful Kotlin standard library through practical code examples

Samuel Urbanowicz

BIRMINGHAM - MUMBAI

Kotlin Standard Library Cookbook

Commissioning Editor: Richa Tripathi
Acquisition Editor: Chaitanya Nair
Content Development Editor: Akshada Iyer
Technical Editor: Abhishek Sharma
Copy Editor: Safis Editing
Project Coordinator: Prajakta Naik
Proofreader: Safis Editing
Indexer: Tejal Daruwale Soni
Graphics: Jisha Chirayil
Production Coordinator: Aparna Bhagat

First published: July 2018

Production reference: 1260718

Published by Packt Publishing Ltd.
Livery Place
35 Livery Street
Birmingham
B3 2PB, UK.

ISBN 978-1-78883-766-8

www.packtpub.com

"I have no special talent. I am only passionately curious."
- A. Einstein

I dedicate the book to all curious souls... most of all to you, Agat.

`mapt.io`

Mapt is an online digital library that gives you full access to over 5,000 books and videos, as well as industry leading tools to help you plan your personal development and advance your career. For more information, please visit our website.

Why subscribe?

- Spend less time learning and more time coding with practical eBooks and Videos from over 4,000 industry professionals

- Improve your learning with Skill Plans built especially for you

- Get a free eBook or video every month

- Mapt is fully searchable

- Copy and paste, print, and bookmark content

PacktPub.com

Did you know that Packt offers eBook versions of every book published, with PDF and ePub files available? You can upgrade to the eBook version at `www.PacktPub.com` and as a print book customer, you are entitled to a discount on the eBook copy. Get in touch with us at `service@packtpub.com` for more details.

At `www.PacktPub.com`, you can also read a collection of free technical articles, sign up for a range of free newsletters, and receive exclusive discounts and offers on Packt books and eBooks.

Contributors

About the author

Samuel Urbanowicz is an experienced software engineer skilled in mobile applications and backend development. A fan of modern programming languages, he has been using Kotlin since its beginning. He's always curious to dive into technologies. He is especially passionate about machine learning. Samuel believes that the Kotlin language has great potential for multiplatform development. He has work experience in both big corps and small start-ups. He is an active contributor to open source projects.

I would like to thank the mentors who inspired me along my programming adventures. I wouldn't have the same passion for programming if not for the wisdom I learned from you: "Coding must be fun, otherwise we are doing it wrong!". I am also grateful to the reviewers who made the book better. This book could not have been written without you.

About the reviewer

Miłosz Pacholczyk is a software developer with 5 years of commercial experience in Java. He worked on B2B software used by leading manufacturers of automotive and construction industries. He graduated from the University of Warsaw.

Packt is searching for authors like you

If you're interested in becoming an author for Packt, please visit `authors.packtpub.com` and apply today. We have worked with thousands of developers and tech professionals, just like you, to help them share their insight with the global tech community. You can make a general application, apply for a specific hot topic that we are recruiting an author for, or submit your own idea.

Table of Contents

Preface

The primary aim of *Kotlin Standard Library Cookbook* is to help you dive into advanced language concepts and features as fast as possible in a friendly way. It covers a wide range of general programming problems at varying difficulty levels, including design patterns, functional programming, data processing, and more. The book consists of recipes that present a specific problem and give a step-by-step explanation of how to approach it effectively. All the presented features of the standard library are well explained, allowing you to discover them with ease.

This book will help software developers switch to Kotlin with ease and integrate it seamlessly into the existing JVM and JavaScript projects. Examples included in the book can easily be implemented in your own projects. You can also get the ready-made solutions from the book's GitHub repository if you prefer to follow and test the recipes in your favorite IDE. Once you have completed the book, you should have expert knowledge and insight into the language's advanced concepts, allowing you to address your daily programming challenges efficiently.

Who this book is for

The book is ideal for those who are already familiar with the basics of Kotlin and want to discover how to effectively solve day-to-day programming problems with state-of-the-art solutions, utilizing advanced language and standard library features. Experienced programmers who are willing to switch to Kotlin from other languages, especially Java, Scala, and JavaScript, will find it helpful as well.

What this book covers

Chapter 1, *Ranges, Progressions, and Sequences,* presents the concept of Kotlin ranges and sequences. It shows how to approach common algorithmic problems by defining custom sequences and how to define ranges for custom classes.

Chapter 2, *Expressive Functions and Adjustable Interfaces,* shows how to approach designing functions and interfaces using the language's built-in features. The chapter explains how to implement clean, reusable functions, and scalable interfaces containing default implementations. The recipes also cover other features of the language, such as inlining closures, destructuring variables, reified type parameters, and other useful tips that help design more flexible and natural code.

Chapter 3, *Shaping Code with Kotlin Functional Programming Features*, shows how to solve real-life programming challenges by adopting state-of-the-art functional programming patterns. The chapter helps readers get familiar with Kotlin support for functional programming concepts provided by the standard library and the built-in language features.

Chapter 4, *Powerful Data Processing*, focuses on presenting standard library support for declarative style operations on collections. The included recipes present solutions to varying programming problems related to dataset transformations, reducing, or filtering. The chapter shows how to approach data processing operations practicing a functional programming style with the use of powerful functionalities built into the standard library.

Chapter 5, *Tasteful Design Patterns Adopting Kotlin Concepts*, presents the Kotlin-specific approach to implementing popular design patterns, including the Observer and Lazy delegates, Builder, Strategy, and more. Design patterns presented in the following chapter are backed by real-life examples that emphasize the benefits of the Delegation pattern.

Chapter 6, *Friendly I/O Operations*, presents useful extension functions available in the standard library that simplify the work with I/O operations. The chapter focuses on common use cases of read-write operations on files, working with streams and buffers, and the Kotlin approach to traversing files available in a specific directory.

Chapter 7, *Making Asynchronous Programming Great Again*, is an in-depth guide to asynchronous programming focusing on the Kotlin coroutines framework and its application in real-life situations. The chapter presents how to optimize and advance previous examples by executing parts of their code in the background in a non-blocking way. Here, you will also find a practical example of implementing an asynchronous REST client with the Retrofit library and the coroutines framework.

Chapter 8, *Best Practices for the Android, JUnit, and JVM UI Frameworks*, covers practical problems specific to the popular frameworks, among which Kotlin is the one used most often. In general, it will focus on Android platform-specific aspects and asynchronous UI programming with coroutines, both on Android and JVM frameworks such as JavaFX and Swing. It will also help you to write effective unit tests for the JVM platform using the JUnit framework. The recipes related to unit testing will also include more advanced topics, such as mocking dependencies with the Mockito Kotlin library and testing asynchronous code based on the coroutines framework.

Chapter 9, *Miscellaneous*, presents handy solutions to various problems and issues that Kotlin developers deal with on a daily basis.

To get the most out of this book

In order to learn from the book efficiently, you should follow the included recipes step by step and try to implement the solutions on your own. You can download the sample code from the book's GitHub repository at `https://github.com/PacktPublishing/Kotlin-Standard-Library-Cookbook` and import it into IntelliJ IDEA and Android Studio. If you have any trouble, you can run and test each recipe instantly in the IDE.

Download the example code files

You can download the example code files for this book from your account at `www.packtpub.com`. If you purchased this book elsewhere, you can visit `www.packtpub.com/support` and register to have the files emailed directly to you.

You can download the code files by following these steps:

1. Log in or register at `www.packtpub.com`.
2. Select the **SUPPORT** tab.
3. Click on **Code Downloads & Errata**.
4. Enter the name of the book in the **Search** box and follow the onscreen instructions.

Once the file is downloaded, please make sure that you unzip or extract the folder using the latest version of:

- WinRAR/7-Zip for Windows
- Zipeg/iZip/UnRarX for Mac
- 7-Zip/PeaZip for Linux

The code bundle for the book is also hosted on GitHub at `https://github.com/PacktPublishing/Kotlin-Standard-Library-Cookbook`. In case there's an update to the code, it will be updated on the existing GitHub repository.

We also have other code bundles from our rich catalog of books and videos available at `https://github.com/PacktPublishing/`. Check them out!

Conventions used

There are a number of text conventions used throughout this book.

CodeInText: Indicates code words in text, database table names, folder names, filenames, file extensions, pathnames, dummy URLs, user input, and Twitter handles. Here is an example: "We can do so with the extension function provided for the IntProgression, LongProgression, and CharProgression types, which is called reversed()."

A block of code is set as follows:

```
val daysOfYear: IntRange = 1..365
for(day in daysOfYear.reversed()) {
    println("Remaining days: $day")
}
```

When we wish to draw your attention to a particular part of a code block, the relevant lines or items are set in bold:

```
val sequence = sequenceOf("a", "b", "c", "d", "e", "f", "g", "h")
val transformedSequence = sequence.map {
    println("Applying map function for $it")
    it
}
```

Any command-line input or output is written as follows:

```
[10, 9, 8, 7, 6, 5, 4, 3, 2, 1, 0]
```

Bold: Indicates a new term, an important word, or words that you see onscreen.

Warnings or important notes appear like this.

Tips and tricks appear like this.

Sections

In this book, you will find several headings that appear frequently (*Getting ready, How to do it..., How it works..., There's more...,* and *See also*).

To give clear instructions on how to complete a recipe, use these sections as follows:

Getting ready

This section tells you what to expect in the recipe and describes how to set up any software or any preliminary settings required for the recipe.

How to do it...

This section contains the steps required to follow the recipe.

How it works...

This section usually consists of a detailed explanation of what happened in the previous section.

There's more...

This section consists of additional information about the recipe in order to make you more knowledgeable about the recipe.

See also

This section provides helpful links to other useful information for the recipe.

Get in touch

Feedback from our readers is always welcome.

General feedback: Email `feedback@packtpub.com` and mention the book title in the subject of your message. If you have questions about any aspect of this book, please email us at `questions@packtpub.com`.

Errata: Although we have taken every care to ensure the accuracy of our content, mistakes do happen. If you have found a mistake in this book, we would be grateful if you would report this to us. Please visit `www.packtpub.com/submit-errata`, selecting your book, clicking on the Errata Submission Form link, and entering the details.

Piracy: If you come across any illegal copies of our works in any form on the Internet, we would be grateful if you would provide us with the location address or website name. Please contact us at `copyright@packtpub.com` with a link to the material.

If you are interested in becoming an author: If there is a topic that you have expertise in and you are interested in either writing or contributing to a book, please visit `authors.packtpub.com`.

Reviews

Please leave a review. Once you have read and used this book, why not leave a review on the site that you purchased it from? Potential readers can then see and use your unbiased opinion to make purchase decisions, we at Packt can understand what you think about our products, and our authors can see your feedback on their book. Thank you!

For more information about Packt, please visit `packtpub.com`.

1
Ranges, Progressions, and Sequences

In this chapter, we will cover the following recipes:

- Exploring the use of range expressions to iterate through alphabet characters
- Traversing through ranges using progression with a custom step value
- Building custom progressions to traverse dates
- Using range expressions with flow control statements
- Discovering the concept of sequences
- Applying sequences to solve algorithmic problems

Introduction

This chapter will focus on explaining the advantages of **range expressions** and **sequences**. These powerful data structure concepts offered by the Kotlin standard library can help you to improve the quality and readability of your code, as well as its safety and performance. Range expressions provide a declarative way of iterating through sets of comparable types using `for` loops. They are also useful for implementing concise and safe control flow statements and conditions. The `Sequence` class, as a missing supplement to the `Collection` type, provides a built-in lazy evaluation of its elements. In many cases, using sequences can help optimize data-processing operations and make the code more efficient in terms of computation complexity and memory consumption. The recipes covered in this chapter are going to focus on solving real-life programming problems. Moreover, at the same time, they are also going to explain how those concepts work under the hood.

Exploring the use of range expressions to iterate through alphabet characters

Ranges, provided by the Kotlin standard library, are a powerful solution for implementing iteration and conditional statements in a natural and safe way. A range can be understood as an abstract data type that represents a set of iterable elements and allows iteration through them in a declarative way. The `ClosedRange` interface from the `kotlin.ranges` package is a basic model of the range data structure. It contains references to the first and last elements of the range and provides the `contains(value: T): Boolean` and `isEmpty(): Boolean` functions, which are responsible for checking whether the specified element belongs to the range and whether the range is empty. In this recipe, we are going to learn how to declare a range that consists of alphabet characters and iterate through it in a decreasing order.

Getting ready

The Kotlin standard library provides functions that allow the declaration of ranges for the integral, primitive types, such as `Int`, `Long`, and `Char`. To define a new range instance, we can use the `rangeTo()` function. For example, we can declare a range of integers from `0` to `1000` in the following way:

```
val range: IntRange = 0.rangeTo(1000)
```

The `rangeTo()` function has also its own special operator equivalent, `..`, which allows the declaration of a range with a more natural syntax:

```
val range: IntRange = 0..1000
```

Also, in order to declare a range of elements in a decreasing order, we can use the `downTo()` function.

How to do it...

1. Declare a decreasing range of alphabet characters:

    ```
    'Z' downTo 'A'
    ```

2. Create a `for` loop to traverse the range:

    ```
    for (letter in 'Z' downTo 'A') print(letter)
    ```

How it works...

As a result, we are going to get the following code printed out to the console:

```
ZYXWVUTSRQPONMLKJIHGFEDCBA
```

As you can see, there is also a `downTo()` extension function variant for the available `Char` type. We are using it to create a range of characters from `Z` to `A`. Note that, thanks for the infix notation, we can omit the brackets while invoking the function—`'Z' downTo 'A'`.

Next, we are creating a `for` loop, which iterates through the range and prints out the subsequent `Char` elements. Using the `in` operator, we are specifying the object that is being iterated in the loop—and that's it! As you can see, the Kotlin syntax for the `for` loop is neat and natural to use.

 Implementations of ranges of the primitive types, such as `IntRange`, `LongRange`, and `CharRange`, also contain `Iterator` interface implementations under the hood. They are being used while traversing the range using the `for` loop under the hood. In fact, the range implementing the `Iterable` interface is called a **progression**. Under the hood, the `IntRange`, `LongRange`, and `CharRange` classes inherit from the `IntProgression`, `LongProgression`, and `CharProgression` base classes, and they provide the implementations of the `Iterator` interface internally.

There's more...

There is also a convenient way to reverse the order of an already-defined progression. We can do so with the extension function provided for the `IntProgression`, `LongProgression`, and `CharProgression` types, which is called `reversed()`. It returns new instances of progressions with a reversed order of elements. Here is an example of how to use the `reversed()` function:

```
val daysOfYear: IntRange = 1..365
for(day in daysOfYear.reversed()) {
    println("Remaining days: $day")
}
```

The preceding `for` loop prints the following text to the console:

```
Remaining days: 365
Remaining days: 364
Remaining days: 363
...
Remaining days: 2
Remaining days: 1
```

The Kotlin standard library offers also another handy extension function called `until()`, which allows the declaration of ranges that don't include the last element. It is pretty useful when working with classes that contain internal collections and don't provide elegant interfaces to access them. A good example would be the Android `ViewGroup` class, which is a container for the child `View` type objects. The following example presents how to iterate through the next indexes of any given `ViewGroup` instance children in order to modify the state of each of the children:

```
val container: ViewGroup = activity.findViewById(R.id.container) as
ViewGroup
(0 until container.childCount).forEach {
    val child: View = container.getChildAt(it)
    child.visibility = View.INVISIBLE
}
```

The `until()` infix function helps to make the loop conditions clean and natural to understand.

See also

- This recipe gave us an insight into how Kotlin standard library implementations of ranges for primitives are easy to work with. A problem can appear if we want to traverse non-primitive types using the `for` loop. However, it turns out we can easily declare a range for any `Comparable` type. This will be shown in the *Building custom progressions to traverse dates* recipe.

- As you have noticed, we are using the `in` operator to specify the object that is being iterated in the loop. However, there are also other scenarios where the `in` and `!in` operators can be used together with ranges. We will investigate them in more depth in the *Using range expressions with flow control statements* recipe.

Traversing through ranges using progression with a custom step value

Besides doing so for the `Iterator` instances, progressions implementations for integral types, such as the `Int`, `Long`, and `Char` types, also include the `step` property. The `step` value specifies the intervals between the subsequent elements of a range. By default, the `step` value of a progression is equal to 1. In this recipe, we are going to learn how to traverse a range of alphabet characters with a `step` value equal to 2. In the result, we want to have every second alphabet letter printed to the console.

Getting ready

The Kotlin standard library provides a convenient way of creating progression with a custom `step` value. We can do so using an extension function for progressions of integral types called `step()`. We can also benefit from the infix notation and declare a progression with a custom `step`, as follows:

```
val progression: IntProgression = 0..1000 step 100
```

If we were to use `progression` in the `for` loop, it would iterate 10 times:

```
val progression: IntProgression = 0..1000 step 100
for (i in progression) {
    println(i)
}
```

We could also achieve the same result by iterating with the `while` loop, as follows:

```
var i = 0
while (i <= 1000) {
    println(i)
    i += 100
}
```

How to do it...

1. Declare a range of the `Char` type using the `downTo()` function:

   ```
   'z' downTo 'a'
   ```

2. Convert the range to a progression with a custom `step` value using the `step()` function:

   ```
   'z' downTo 'a' step 2
   ```

3. Use the `forEach()` function to iterate through the elements of the progression and print each of them to the console:

   ```
   ('z' downTo 'a' step 2).forEach { character -> print(character) }
   ```

How it works...

In the result, we are going to get the following code printed to the console:

```
zxvtrpnljhfdb
```

In the beginning, we declared a range containing all the alphabet characters in decreasing order with the `downTo()` function. Then, we transformed the range a the custom progression containing every second character with the `step()` function. Finally, we are using the `Iterable.forEach()` function to iterate through the next elements of the progression and print each of them to the console.

The `step()` extension function is available for the `IntProgression`, `LongProgression`, and `CharProgression` types. Under the hood, it creates a new instance of a progression copying the properties of the original one and setting up the new `step` value.

See also

- Apart from iteration, range expressions are useful for defining flow control conditions. You can read more about this in the *Using range expressions with flow control statements* recipe.

Building custom progressions to traverse dates

Kotlin provides built-in support for ranges of primitive types. In the previous recipes, we worked with the IntRange and CharRange types, which are included in the Kotlin standard library. However, it is possible to implement a custom progression for any type by implementing the Comparable interface. In this recipe, we will learn how to create a progression of the LocalDate type and discover how to traverse the dates the easy way.

Getting ready

In order to accomplish the task, we need to start by getting familiar with the ClosedRange and Iterator interfaces. We need to use them to declare a custom progression for the LocalDate class:

```
public interface ClosedRange<T: Comparable<T>> {
    public val start: T
    public val endInclusive: T
    public operator fun contains(value: T): Boolean {
        return value >= start && value <= endInclusive
    }
    public fun isEmpty(): Boolean = start > endInclusive
}
```

The Iterator interface provides information about the subsequent values and their availability:

```
public interface Iterator<out T> {
    public operator fun next(): T
    public operator fun hasNext(): Boolean
}
```

The ClosedRange interface provides the minimum and maximum values of the range. It also provides the contains(value: T): Boolean and isEmpty(): Boolean functions, which check whether a given value belongs to the range and whether the range is empty respectively. Those two functions have default implementations provided in the ClosedRange interface. As the result, we don't need to override them in our custom implementation of the ClosedRange interface.

How to do it...

1. Let's start with implementing the `Iterator` interface for the `LocalDate` type. We are going to create a custom `LocalDateIterator` class, which implements the `Iterator<LocalDate>` interface:

```
class DateIterator(startDate: LocalDate,
                   val endDateInclusive: LocalDate,
                   val stepDays: Long) : Iterator<LocalDate> {
    private var currentDate = startDate
    override fun hasNext() = currentDate <= endDateInclusive
    override fun next(): LocalDate {
        val next = currentDate
        currentDate = currentDate.plusDays(stepDays)
        return next
    }
}
```

2. Now, we can implement the progression for the `LocalDate` type. Let's create a new class called `DateProgression`, which is going to implement the `Iterable<LocalDate>` and `ClosedRange<LocalDate>` interfaces:

```
class DateProgression(override val start: LocalDate,
                      override val endInclusive: LocalDate,
                      val stepDays: Long = 1) :
Iterable<LocalDate>,
ClosedRange<LocalDate> {
    override fun iterator(): Iterator<LocalDate> {
        return DateIterator(start, endInclusive, stepDays)
    }

    infix fun step(days: Long) = DateProgression(start,
endInclusive, days)
}
```

3. Finally, declare a custom `rangeTo` operator for the `LocalDate` class:

```
operator fun LocalDate.rangeTo(other: LocalDate) =
DateProgression(this, other)
```

How it works...

Now, we are able to declare range expressions for the `LocalDate` type. Let's see how to use our implementation. In the following example, we will use our custom `LocalDate.rangeTo` operator implementation in order to create a range of dates and iterate its elements:

```
val startDate = LocalDate.of(2020, 1, 1)
val endDate = LocalDate.of(2020, 12, 31)
for (date in startDate..endDate step 7) {
    println("${date.dayOfWeek} $date ")
}
```

As a result, we are going to have the dates printed out to the console with a week-long interval:

```
WEDNESDAY 2020-01-01
WEDNESDAY 2020-01-08
WEDNESDAY 2020-01-15
WEDNESDAY 2020-01-22
WEDNESDAY 2020-01-29
WEDNESDAY 2020-02-05
...
WEDNESDAY 2020-12-16
WEDNESDAY 2020-12-23
WEDNESDAY 2020-12-30
```

The `DateIterator` class holds three properties—`currentDate: LocalDate`, `endDateInclusive: LocalDate`, and `stepDays: Long`. In the beginning, the `currentDate` property is initialized with the `startDate` value passed in the constructor. Inside the `next()` function, we are returning the `currentDate` value and updating it to the next date value using a given `stepDays` property interval.

The `DateProgression` class combines the functionalities of the `Iterable<LocalDate>` and `ClosedRange<LocalDate>` interfaces. It provides the `Iterator` object required by the `Iterable` interface by returning the `DateIterator` instance. It also overrides the `start` and `endInclusive` properties of the `ClosedRange` interface. There is also the `stepDays` property with a default value equal to 1. Note that every time the `step` function is called, a new instance of the `DateProgression` class is being created.

You can follow the same pattern to implement custom progressions for any class that implements the `Comparable` interface.

Using range expressions with flow control statements

Apart from iterations, Kotlin range expressions can be useful when it comes to working with control flow statements. In this recipe, we are going to learn how to use range expressions together with `if` and `when` statements in order to tune up the code and make it safe. In this recipe, we are going to consider an example of using the `in` operator to define a condition of an `if` statement.

Getting ready

Kotlin range expressions—represented by the `ClosedRange` interface—implement a `contains(value: T): Boolean` function, which returns an information if a given parameter belongs to the range. This feature makes it convenient to use ranges together with control flow instructions. The `contains()` function has also its equivalent operator, `in`, and its negation, `!in`.

How to do it...

1. Let's create a variable and assign to it a random integer value:

```
val randomInt = Random().nextInt()
```

2. Now we can check whether the `randomInt` value belongs to the scope of integers from 0 to 10 inclusive using range expressions:

```
if (randomInt in 0..10) {
    print("$randomInt belongs to <0, 10> range")
} else {
    print("$randomInt doesn't belong to <0, 10> range")
}
```

How it works...

We have used a range expression together with the in operator in order to define a condition for the if statement. The condition statement is natural to read and concise. In contrast, an equivalent classic implementation would look like this:

```
val randomInt = Random(20).nextInt()
if (randomInt >= 0 && randomInt <= 10) {
    print("$randomInt belongs to <0, 10> range")
} else {
    print("$randomInt doesn't belong to <0, 10> range")
}
```

No doubt, the declarative approach using the range and in operator is cleaner and easier to read, compared to classic, imperative-style condition statements.

There's more...

Range expressions can enhance use of the when expression as well. In the following example, we are going to implement a simple function that will be responsible for mapping a student's exam score to a corresponding grade. Let's say we have the following enum class model for student grades:

```
enum class Grade { A, B, C, D }
```

We can define a function that will map the exam score value, in the 0 to 100 % range, to the proper grade (A, B, C, or D) using a when expression, as follows:

```
fun computeGrade(score: Int): Grade =
        when (score) {
            in 90..100 -> Grade.A
            in 75 until 90 -> Grade.B
            in 60 until 75 -> Grade.C
            in 0 until 60 -> Grade.D
            else -> throw IllegalStateException("Wrong score value!")
        }
```

Using ranges together with the in operator makes the implementation of the computeGrade() function much cleaner and more natural than the classic equivalent implementation using traditional comparison operators, such as <, >, <=, and >=.

See also

- If you'd like to discover more about lambdas, the infix notation, and operator overloading, go ahead and dive into Chapter 2, *Expressive Functions and Adjustable Interfaces*

Discovering the concept of sequences

In terms of high-level functionalities, the Sequence and Collection data structures are nearly the same. They both allow iteration through their elements. There are also many powerful extension functions in the Kotlin standard library that provide declarative-style data-processing operations for each of them. However, the Sequence data structure behaves differently under the hood—it delays any operations on its elements until they are finally consumed. It instantiates the subsequent elements on the go while traversing through them. These characteristics of Sequence, called **lazy evaluation**, make the structure quite similar to the Java concept, Stream. To understand all of this better, we are going to implement a simple data-processing scenario to analyze the efficiency and behavior of Sequence in implementation scenarios, and contrast our findings with Collection-based implementation.

Getting ready

Let's consider the following example:

```
val collection = listOf("a", "b", "c", "d", "e", "f", "g", "h")
val transformedCollection = collection.map {
    println("Applying map function for $it")
    it
}
println(transformedCollection.take(2))
```

In the first line, we created a list of strings and assigned it to the collection variable. Next, we are applying the map() function to the list. Mapping operation allows us to transform each element of the collection and return a new value instead of the original one. In our case, we are using it just to observe that map() was invoked by printing the message to the console. Finally, we want to filter our collection to contain only the first two elements using the take() function and print the content of the list to the console.

In the end, the preceding code prints the following output:

```
Applying map function for a
Applying map function for b
Applying map function for c
Applying map function for d
Applying map function for e
Applying map function for f
Applying map function for g
Applying map function for h
[a, b]
```

As you can see, the map() function was properly applied to every element of the collection and the take() function has properly filtered the elements of the list. However, it would not be an optimal implementation if we were working with a larger dataset. Preferably, we would like to wait with the execution of the data-processing operations until we know what specific elements of the dataset we really need, and then apply those operations only to those elements. It turns out that we can easily optimize our scenario using the Sequence data structure. Let's explore how to do it in the next section.

How to do it...

1. Declare a Sequence instance for the given elements:

   ```
   val sequence = sequenceOf("a", "b", "c", "d", "e", "f", "g", "h")
   ```

2. Apply the mapping operation to the elements of the sequence:

   ```
   val sequence = sequenceOf("a", "b", "c", "d", "e", "f", "g", "h")
   val transformedSequence = sequence.map {
       println("Applying map function for $it")
       it
   }
   ```

3. Print the first two elements of the sequence to the console:

   ```
   val sequence = sequenceOf("a", "b", "c", "d", "e", "f", "g", "h")

   val transformedSequence = sequence.map {
       println("Applying map function for $it")
       it
   }
   println(transformedSequence.take(2).toList())
   ```

How it works...

The `Sequence`-based implementation is going to give us the following output:

```
Applying map function for a
Applying map function for b
[a, b]
```

As you can see, replacing the `Collection` data structure with the `Sequence` type allows us to gain the desired optimization.

The scenario considered in this recipe was implemented identically—first, using `List`, then using the `Sequence` type. However, we can notice the difference in the behavior of the `Sequence` data structure compared to that of `Collection`. The `map()` function was applied only to the first two elements of the sequence, even though the `take()` function was called after the mapping transformation declaration. It's also worth noting that in the example using `Collection`, the mapping was performed instantly when the `map()` function was invoked. In the case of `Sequence`, mapping was performed at the time of the evaluation of its elements while printing them to the console, and more precisely while converting `Sequence` to the `List` type with the following line of code:

```
println(transformedSequence.take(2).toList())
```

There's more...

There is a convenient way of transforming `Collection` to `Sequence`. We can do so with the `asSequence()` extension function provided by the Kotlin standard library for the `Iterable` type. In order to convert a `Sequence` instance into a `Collection` instance, you can use the `toList()` function.

See also

- Thanks to the feature of `Sequence` lazy evaluation, we have avoided needless calculations, increasing the performance of the code at the same time. Lazy evaluation allows the implementation of sequences with a potentially infinite number of elements and turns out to be effective when implementing algorithms as well.

- You can explore a `Sequence`-based implementation of the Fibonacci algorithm in the *Applying sequences to solve algorithmic problems* recipe. It presents, in more detail, another useful function for defining sequences called `generateSequence()`.

Applying sequences to solve algorithmic problems

In this recipe, we are going to get familiar with the `generateSequence()` function, which provides an easy way to define the various types of sequences. We will use it to implement an algorithm for generating Fibonacci numbers.

Getting ready

The basic variant of the `generateSequence()` function is declared as follows:

```
fun <T : Any> generateSequence(nextFunction: () -> T?): Sequence<T>
```

It takes one parameter called `nextFunction`, which is a function that returns the next elements of the sequence. Under the hood, it is being invoked by the `Iterator.next()` function, inside the `Sequence` class' internal implementation, and allows instantiation of the next object to be returned while consuming the sequence values.

In the following example, we are going to implement a finite sequence that emits integers from 10 to 0:

```
var counter = 10
val sequence: Sequence<Int> = generateSequence {
    counter--.takeIf { value: Int -> value >= 0 }
}
print(sequence.toList())
```

The `takeIf()` function applied to the current `counter` value checks whether its value is greater or equal to 0. If the condition is fulfilled, it returns the `counter` value; otherwise, it returns `null`. Whenever `null` is returned by the `generateSequence()` function, the sequence stops. After the `takeIf` function returns the value, the `counter` value is post-decremented. The preceding code will result in the following numbers being printed to the console:

```
[10, 9, 8, 7, 6, 5, 4, 3, 2, 1, 0]
```

The subsequent values of the Fibonacci sequence are generated by summing up their two preceding ones. Additionally, the two first values are equal to 0 and 1. In order to implement such a sequence, we are going to use an extended variant of the `generateSequence()` function with an additional `seed` parameter, declared as follows:

```
fun <T : Any> generateSequence(seed: T?, nextFunction: (T) -> T?):
Sequence<T>
```

How to do it...

1. Declare a function called `fibonacci()` and use the `generateSequence()` function to define a formula for the next elements of the sequence:

```
fun fibonacci(): Sequence<Int> {
    return generateSequence(Pair(0, 1)) { Pair(it.second, it.first
+ it.second) }
            .map { it.first }
}
```

2. Use the `fibonacci()` function to print the next Fibonacci numbers to the console:

```
println(fibonacci().take(20).toList())
```

How it works...

As a result, we are going to get the next 20 Fibonacci numbers printed to the console:

```
[0, 1, 1, 2, 3, 5, 8, 13, 21, 34, 55, 89, 144, 233, 377, 610, 987, 1597,
2584, 4181]
```

The additional `seed` parameter in the `generateSequence()` provides a starting value. The `nextFunction()` function is applied to the `seed` while computing the second value. Later on, it is generating each following element using its preceding value. However, in the case of the Fibonacci sequence, we have two initial values and we need a pair of preceding values in order to compute the next value. For this reason, we wrapped them in `Pair` type instances. Basically, we are defining a sequence of `Pair<Int, Int>` type elements, and in each `nextFunction()` call, we are returning a new pair that holds the values updated accordingly. At the end, we just need to use the `map()` function to replace each `Pair` element with the value of its `first` property. As a result, we are getting an infinite sequence of integer types returning the subsequent Fibonacci numbers.

2
Expressive Functions and Adjustable Interfaces

In this chapter, we will cover the following recipes:

- Declaring adjustable functions with default parameters
- Declaring interfaces containing default implementations
- Extending functionalities of classes
- Destructuring types
- Returning multiple data
- Inlining parameters of closure type
- Infix notations for functions
- Smart types checking with generic reified parameters
- Overloading operators

Introduction

This chapter will focus on exploring a number of Kotlin features that can help to write functions and interfaces that are robust, flexible, and clean. After reading the following recipes, you will understand the language-specific support and approach for boilerplate code reduction and runtime performance improvements. You will also understand the way functions of the standard library are implemented under the hood and how to work with them effectively.

Declaring adjustable functions with default parameters

When creating new functions, we often need to allow some of their parameters to be optional. This forces us to use method overloading to create multiple function declarations with the same name but different sets of arguments related to different use cases and scenarios. Usually, under the hood, each variant of the function is calling the base function with the default implementation. Let's consider a simple example of a function that calculates a displacement of an object moving with a constant acceleration rate:

```
fun calculateDisplacement(initialSpeed: Float,
                          acceleration: Float,
                          duration: Long): Double =
    initialSpeed * duration + 0.5 * acceleration * duration * duration
```

We might also need to provide a displacement calculation for the scenario where the initial speed of the object is always equal to zero. In such a case, we would end up with overloading the basic function in the following manner:

```
fun calculateDisplacement(acceleration: Float, duration: Long): Double =
calculateDisplacement(0f, acceleration, duration)
```

However, Kotlin allows you to reduce multiple declarations and to handle a number of different use cases with a single function having optional parameters. In this recipe, we are going to design an adjustable version of the `calculateDisplacement()` function with an optional `initialSpeed: Float` parameter.

How to do it...

1. Let's declare the basic implementation for the function:

```
fun calculateDisplacement(initialSpeed: Float,
                          acceleration: Float,
                          duration: Long): Double =
    initialSpeed * duration + 0.5 * acceleration * duration *
    duration
```

2. Let's declare a default value for the `initialSpeed` parameter:

```
fun calculateDisplacement(initialSpeed: Float = 0f,
                          acceleration: Float,
```

```
                         duration: Long): Double =
        initialSpeed * duration + 0.5 * acceleration * duration *
        duration
```

How it works...

We've declared a default value for the `initialSpeed` parameter, equal to 0. Once you have a default value assigned, the `initialSpeed` parameter becomes an optional one. We can now omit it while invoking the function, as shown in the following example:

```
val displacement = calculateDisplacement(acceleration = 9.81f, duration =
1000)
```

Note that, if we are omitting some of the parameters and using their default values, we have to specify the values of the other parameters together with their names explicitly. This allows the compiler to map the values to the specific parameters. Of course, we are able to override the default value using the standard way:

```
val displacement = calculateDisplacement(10f, 9.81f, 1000)
```

See also

- Kotlin makes it possible to declare interfaces containing default function implementations. You can learn more about this feature in the *Declaring interfaces containing default implementations* recipe.

Declaring interfaces containing default implementations

Kotlin makes the interface a powerful language element by offering the possibility to declare default implementations for its functions and to define default values of its properties. Those features bring the interface to a whole new level, allowing you to use it for more advanced applications than simple contract declarations.

In this recipe, we are going to define a reusable interface responsible for validating email address values entered by a user into the input field in an abstract registration form. The interface will provide two functions. The first one is responsible for parsing the email address and deciding if the given value is a valid email address, and the second one responsible for extracting a user's login from the email text entered into the form.

Getting ready

The declaration of an interface with a default function implementation is easy. Instead of declaring the function header, we need to include its body too:

```
interface MyInterface {
    fun foo() {
        // default function body
    }
}
```

How to do it...

1. Declare a new interface called `EmailValidator`:

   ```
   interface EmailValidator {}
   ```

2. Add a string property responsible for holding the current text input:

   ```
   interface EmailValidator {
       var input: String
   }
   ```

3. Add the `isEmailValid()` function to the interface:

   ```
   interface EmailValidator {
       var input: String
       fun isEmailValid(): Boolean = input.contains("@")
   }
   ```

4. Add the `getUserLogin()` function:

   ```
   interface EmailValidator {
       var input: String

       fun isEmailValid(): Boolean = input.contains("@")

       fun getUserLogin(): String =
           if (isEmailValid()) {
               input.substringBefore("@")
           } else {
               ""
           }
   }
   ```

How it works...

Now, let's give it a try and take a look at how we can use the `EmailValidator` interface in action. Let's assume we have a `RegistrationForm` class containing a hook method that is invoked every time the input text is modified:

```
class RegistrationForm() {
    fun onInputTextUpdated(text: String) {
        // do some actions on text changed
    }
}
```

To make use of our `EmailValidator` interface, we need to declare a class that is implementing it. We can modify the `RegistrationForm` class to implement the `EmailValidator` interface:

```
class RegistrationForm(override var input: String = ""): EmailValidator {
    fun onInputTextUpdated(newText: String) {
        this.input = newText

        if (!isEmailValid()) {
            print("Wait! You've entered wrong email...")
        } else {
            print("Email is correct, thanks: ${getUserLogin()}!")
        }
    }
}
```

Every time the `onInputUpdated()` function is invoked, we are updating the `input: String` property declared in the `EmailValidator` interface. Once it is up to date, we are using the `EmailValidator` interface functions `isEmailValid()` and `getUserLogin()` values. Extracting the function implementations to the interface makes it possible to reuse them and integrate them easily in a number of classes. The only part that needs an actual implementation is the `input` property of the `EmailValidator` interface, which holds the current state of the text inserted by the user. The smooth way of integrating the `EmailValidator` interface makes it great when it comes to reusability and versatility of the application in different scenarios.

There's more...

It's important to keep in mind that, although we can define a default function implementation in the interface, we are not able to instantiate default values for interface properties. Unlike the class properties, properties of an interface are abstract. They don't have backing fields that could hold a current value (state). If we declare a property inside an interface, we need to implement it in the class or object that implements this interface. This is the main difference between interfaces and abstract classes. Abstract classes can have constructors and can store properties along with their implementations.

As with Java, we can't extend multiple classes; however, we can implement multiple interfaces. When we have a class implementing multiple interfaces containing default implementations, we are at risk of dealing with conflicts caused by functions having the same signatures:

```
interface A {
    fun foo() {
        // some operations
    }
}

interface B {
    fun foo() {
        // other operations
    }
}
```

In this case, we need to override the `foo()` function explicitly to resolve the conflict:

```
class MyClass: A, B {
    override fun foo() {
        print("I'm the first one here!")
    }
}
```

Otherwise, we would get the following error:

Class 'MyClass' must override public open fun foo(): Unit because it inherits multiple interface methods of it.

See also

- A similar feature of Kotlin is the ability to declare default values of functions' parameters. You can learn more about it in the *Declaring adjustable functions with default parameters* recipe.

Extending functionalities of classes

While working on implementing new features or refactoring of existing code, we often end up extracting some part of the code to functions in order to reuse them in different places. If the extracted function is atomic enough, we often end up exporting it to external utility classes whose primary purpose is to extend functionalities of existing classes. Kotlin provides an interesting alternative to the utility classes. It offers a built-in feature allowing us to extend functionalities of other classes with *extension functions* and *extension properties*.

In this recipe, we are going to extend the functionality of the Array<T> class and add a swap(a:T, b: T) extension function to it, which is responsible for changing places of a two given elements of the array.

Getting ready

We can declare extension functions and extension properties inside any file in the project. However, to keep them well organized, it's better to put them in dedicated files.

The syntax for extension functions is very similar to the one of the standard function. We just need to add information about the type that is being extended with the new function, as follows:

```
fun SomeClass.newFunctionName(args): ReturnType {
    // body
}
```

How to do it...

1. Create a new file, Extensions.kt, to store the extension function definition.
2. Implement the swap() function inside:

```
fun <T> Array<T>.swap(a: T, b: T) {
    val positionA = indexOf(a)
```

```
            val positionB = indexOf(b)

            if (positionA < 0 || positionB < 0) {
                throw IllegalArgumentException("Given param doesn't belong
                to the array")
            }

            val tmp = this[positionA]
            this[positionA] = this[positionB]
            this[positionB] = tmp
        }
```

How it works...

As a result, we are able to call the `swap` function on any instance of the `Array` class. Let's consider the following example:

```
val array: Array<String> = arrayOf("a", "b", "c", "d")
array.swap("c", "b")
print(array.joinToString())
```

This results in printing the following output to the console:

```
a, c, b, d
```

As you can see, we can access the current instance of the class inside the extension function using the `this` keyword.

There's more...

Apart from extension functions, Kotlin also offers an extension properties feature. For example, we can declare a property for the `List<T>` class that will hold information about the last element index value:

```
val <T> List<T>.lastIndex: Int  get() = size - 1
```

Extensions are a widely used pattern across Kotlin standard library classes. They work seamlessly with Java, Kotlin, JavaScript, and native classes defined within the project and in external dependencies as well.

Destructuring types

It is often practical to convert a single object of a complex type into a number of variables. This allows you to provide proper naming for the variables and simplifies the code. Kotlin provides an easy, built-in way to achieve this with a feature called *destructuring*:

```
data class User(val login: String, val email: String, val birthday:
LocalDate)

fun getUser() = User("Agata", "ag@t.pl", LocalDate.of(1990, 1, 18))

val (name, mail, birthday) = getUser()

print("$name was born on $birthday")
```

As a result, this piece of code would print the following message to the console:

Agata was born on 1990-01-18

Pretty awesome! Destructuring is available for data classes out of the box. The Kotlin standard library provides this feature for many common types as well. However, destructuring is not available explicitly whenever we are dealing with custom, non-data classes. Especially, while working with classes from external libraries written in other languages such as Java, we need to define the destructuring mechanism manually. In this recipe, we are going to implement destructuring for a Java class defined as follows:

```java
// Java code
public class LightBulb {
    private final int id;
    private boolean turnedOn = false;

    public LightBulb(int id) {
        this.id = id;
    }

    public void setTurnedOn(boolean turnedOn) {
        this.turnedOn = turnedOn;
    }

    public boolean getTurnedOn() {
        return turnedOn;
    }
    public int getId() {
        return id;
    }
}
```

Getting ready

Destructuring declarations in Kotlin are position-based, opposed to property name-based declarations available in other languages. This means the Kotlin compiler decides which class property is linked to which variable based on the order of the properties. In order to allow custom class destructuring, we need to add implementations of the functions called `componentN`, where *N* refers to the component number marked with the `operator` keyword to allow using them in a destructuring declaration.

How to do it...

1. Declare an extension function returning the `id` property of the `LightBulb` class:

   ```
   operator fun LightBulb.component1() = this.id
   ```

2. Add another extension `componentN` function responsible for returning the `turnedOn` property:

   ```
   operator fun LightBulb.component2() = this.turnedOn
   ```

How it works...

Once we declare proper `componentN` functions, we can benefit from destructuring of the `LightBulb` type objects:

```
val (id, turnedOn) = LightBulb(1)
print("Light bulb number $id is turned ${if (turnedOn) "on" else "off"}")
```

This code would print the following output to the console:

```
Light bulb number 1 is turned off
```

As you can see, the `component1()` function was assigned to the first variable of the destructured declaration—`id`. Similarly, the second `turnedOn` variable was assigned with the result of the `component2()` function.

There's more...

Because of the fact that properties in destructured object assignments are position-based, sometimes we are forced to declare more variables than we want to use. We can use an underscore if we don't need to use a certain value, avoiding the compiler hint indicating an unused variable and simplifying the code a bit:

```
val (_, turnedOn) = LightBulb(1)
print("Light bulb is turned ${if (turnedOn) "on" else "off"}")
```

Destructuring is also available for function return values:

```
val (login, domain) = "agata@magdalena.com".split("@")
print("login: $login, domain: $domain")
```

The preceding code is going to return the following output:

login: agata, domain: magdalena.com

We can also use destructured declarations with lambda expressions:

```
listOf(LightBulb(0), LightBulb(1))
        .filter { (_, isOn) -> isOn }
        .map { (id, _) -> id }
```

Another useful application of destructured declarations is an iteration. For example, we can use this feature to traverse through map entries:

```
val lightBulbsWithNames =
        mapOf(LightBulb(0) to "Bedroom", LightBulb(1) to "Kitchen")

for ((lightbulb, name) in lightBulbsWithNames) {
    lightbulb.turnedOn = true
}
```

Returning multiple data

Although Kotlin doesn't provide a multiple return feature, thanks to data classes and destructuring declarations, it is quite convenient to write functions that return a number of values of different types. In this recipe, we are going to implement a function returning the result of dividing two numbers. The result is going to contain the quotient and remainder values.

How to do it...

1. Let's start with declaring a data class for the return type:

    ```
    data class DivisionResult(val quotient: Int, val remainder: Int)
    ```

2. Let's implement the `divide()` function:

    ```
    fun divide(dividend: Int, divisor: Int): DivisionResult {
        val quotient = dividend.div(divisor)
        val remainder = dividend.rem(divisor)
        return DivisionResult(quotient, remainder)
    }
    ```

How it works...

We can see the `divide()` function in action:

```
val dividend = 10
val divisor = 3
val (quotient, remainder) = divide(dividend, divisor)

print("$dividend / $divisor = $quotient r $remainder")
```

The preceding code is going to print the following output:

```
10 / 3 = 3 r 1
```

Thanks to the fact that we are returning a data class instance, the `DivisionResult` class, we can benefit from the destructuring feature and assign the result to a set of separate variables.

There's more...

The Kotlin standard library provides ready to use `Pair` and `Triple` classes. We can use them to return two and three values of any type. This eliminates the need to create a dedicated data classes for the return type. On the other hand, using data classes gives us the ability to operate on more meaningful names, which adds more clarity to the code.

The following example demonstrates using the `Pair` class to return two objects at the same time:

```
fun getBestScore(): Pair<String, Int> = Pair("Max", 1000)
val (name, score) = getBestScore()
print("User $name has the best score of $score points")
```

See also

- If you'd like to get more familiar with destructuring declarations, you can take a look at the *Destructuring types* recipe

Inlining parameters of closure type

Usage of higher-order functions can lead to a decrease of runtime performance. Memory allocations of the functions passed as lambda arguments and their virtual calls in a function body lead to runtime overhead. However, in many cases, we can eliminate this type of overhead by inlining the lambda expression parameters.

In this recipe, we are going to implement the `lock()` function that will automate work with the Java `java.util.concurrent.locks.Lock` interface. The function will take two arguments—an instance of the `Lock` interface and the function that should be invoked after the lock is acquired. Finally, our `lock()` function should release the lock. We also want to allow making the function parameter inlined.

Getting ready

To declare an inline function, we simply need to add the `inline` modifier in front of the function header.

How to do it...

Let's declare a `lock()` function with two arguments—an instance of the `Lock` interface and the function to be invoked after the lock is acquired:

```
inline fun performHavingLock(lock: Lock, task: () -> Unit) {
    lock.lock()
    try {
```

```
        task()
    }
    finally {
        lock.unlock()
    }
}
```

How it works...

The `performHavingLock()` function allows us to provide synchronization for the function passed to it as the `task` parameter:

```
performHavingLock(ReentrantLock()) {
  print("Wait for it!")
}
```

As a result, the `performHavingLock()` function is going to print the following output to the console:

Wait for it!

Under the hood, the inline modifier affects both the function itself and the lambda expressions passed to it. They are all going to be inlined in the underlying generated bytecode:

```
Lock lock = (Lock)(new ReentrantLock());
lock.lock();

try {
    String var2 = "Wait for it!";
    System.out.print(var2);
} finally {
    lock.unlock();
}
```

If we did not use the `inline` modifier, the compiler would create a separate instance of the `Function0` type in order to pass the lambda argument to the `performHavingLock()` function. Inlining lambdas may cause the generated code to grow. However, if we do it in a reasonable way (that is, avoiding inlining large functions), it will pay off in performance.

There's more...

If you want only some of the lambdas passed to the function to be inlined, you can mark some of the function parameters with the `noinline` modifier:

```
inline fun foo(inlined: () -> Unit, noinline notInlined: () -> Unit) {
    // ...
}
```

Kotlin also allows declaring inline class properties. The `inline` modifier can be used with getter and setter methods of properties that don't have a backing field. For example:

```
val foo: Foo
    inline get() = Foo()

var bar: Bar
    get() = ...
    inline set(v) { ... }
```

We can also annotate an entire property:

```
inline var bar: Bar
    get() = ...
    set(v) { ... }
```

As a result, the inlined getters and setters are going to be represented in the same way as the regular inline functions.

Infix notations for functions

To bring our code closer to the natural language, Kotlin provides infix notations for the functions containing a single parameter. This way, we can invoke the function without using brackets. In this recipe, we are going to learn how to design an infix extension function for the `String` type, named `concat()`, which is responsible for the concatenation of two string values.

Getting ready

In order to enable an infix notation for the function, we simply need to add the `infix` keyword before the function header.

How to do it...

Declare the `concat()` extension function and implement its body:

```
infix fun String.concat(next: String): String = this + next
```

How it works...

Let's test the `concat()` function by running the following code:

```
print("This" concat "is" concat "weird")
```

Great! We have just printed out the following text to the console:

```
Thisisweird
```

There's more...

The Kotlin standard library uses the infix notation extensively. You can benefit from infix functions to shape your code the clean way. One infix function worth noting is the `to()` extension function provided for the `Map.Entry<K, V>` class, which allows you to declare map entries in a minimalistic way:

```
val namesWithBirthdays: Map<String, LocalDate> =
        mapOf("Agata" to LocalDate.of(1990, 1, 18))
```

The `to()` extension function is declared for a generic type `A` and generic argument of type `B`, which returns an instance of a `Pair<A, B>` class.

There are plenty of other functions supporting infix notations available in the standard library. If you check the implementation of the ones you are using on a daily basis, it may turn out they are available in the infix form too.

See also

- You can learn about another cool feature that helps to shape the code to be more natural to read in the *Overloading operators* recipe

Smart types checking with generic reified parameters

While implementing functions that support generic type arguments, we often deal with the need to provide additional information about object types at runtime. On the JVM platform, types have their representations in the Class<T> class instances. For example, we can face such a need while parsing JSON formatted data to the Kotlin class instances using the Gson library:

```
data class ApiResponse(val gifsWithPandas: List<ByteArray>)
data class Error(val message: String)

fun parseJsonResponse(json: String): ApiResponse {
    Gson().fromJson(json, ApiResponse::class.java)
}
```

Normally, we can't access the generic type argument at runtime because of a JVM types erasure. However, Kotlin allows you to overcome this limitation because it preserves the type argument at runtime. In this recipe, we are going to tune up Gson's fromJson(json: String, Class<T>) function to get rid of the additional type argument.

Getting ready

Make sure you have the Gson dependency included in your project (https://github.com/google/gson). If you are using Gradle, build script that you can fetch it with the following declaration:

```
dependencies {
    compile 'com.google.code.gson:gson:2.8.2'
}
```

In order to make a type argument accessible at runtime, we need to mark it with the reified modifier and mark the function as inline.

How to do it...

1. Create a new file where we will put an extension function implementation (for example, GsonExtensions.kt)

2. Inside the file, declare an extension function for the `Gson` class:

```
inline fun <reified T> Gson.fromJson(json: String): T {
    return fromJson(json, T::class.java)
}
```

How it works...

We have implemented an extension function for the `Gson` type. Thanks to adding the `reified` modifier, we can access the generic type argument at runtime and pass it to the original `fromGson()` function.

As a result, we are able to use the more elegant version of the `fromGson()` function in our code:

```
data class ApiResponse(val gifsWithPandas: List<ByteArray>)

val response = Gson().fromJson<ApiResponse>(json)
```

We could also benefit from Kotlin smart casting and omit the explicit type declaration from the function call:

```
val response: ApiResponse = Gson().fromJson(json)
```

Overloading operators

The Kotlin language provides a set of operators which have their own symbol (for example, +, −, *, or /) and a priority defined. At the time of compilation, the Kotlin compiler transforms them into associated function calls or even more complex statements. We are also able to override an operator and declare its custom underlying implementation for a specified type. This implementation would be applied to the instances of the specified type the operator was used with.

In this recipe, we are going to define a class called `Position`, representing the current coordinates of the point in a three-dimensional space. Then, we are going to implement custom `plus` and `minus` operators for our class to provide a simple way of applying a geometric transformation to its instances. As a result, we want to be able to update the coordinates of the point represented by the `Position` class using the + and − operator symbols.

Getting ready

In order to overload the operator for the specific type, we need to provide a member function or an extension function with a fixed name corresponding to the operator. Additionally, functions that overload operators need to be marked with the `operator` keyword.

In the following tables, you can find grouped sets of operators available in the language with their corresponding expressions to which they are translated to:

Unary prefix

Operator	Expression
+a	a.unaryPlus()
-a	a.unaryMinus()
!a	a.not()

Incrementation and decrementation

Operator	Expression
a++	a.inc()
a--	a.dec()

Arithmetic

Operator	Expression
a + b	a.plus(b)
a - b	a.minus(b)
a * b	a.times(b)
a / b	a.div(b)
a % b	a.rem(b)
a..b	a.rangeTo(b)

In operator

Operator	Expression
a in b	b.contains(a)
a !in b	!b.contains(a)

Indexed access

Operator	Expression
a[i]	a.get(i)
a[i, j]	a.get(i, j)
a[i_1, ..., i_n]	a.get(i_1, ..., i_n)
a[i] = b	a.set(i, b)
a[i, j] = b	a.set(i, j, b)
a[i_1, ..., i_n] = b	a.set(i_1, ..., i_n, b)

Invoke operator

Operator	Expression
a()	a.invoke()
a(i)	a.invoke(i)
a(i, j)	a.invoke(i, j)
a(i_1, ..., i_n)	a.invoke(i_1, ..., i_n)

Augmented assignment

Operator	Expression
a += b	a.plusAssign(b)
a -= b	a.minusAssign(b)
a *= b	a.timesAssign(b)
a /= b	a.divAssign(b)
a %= b	a.remAssign(b)

Equality and comparison

Operator	Expression
a == b	a?.equals(b) ?: (b === null)
a != b	!(a?.equals(b) ?: (b === null))
a > b	a.comareTo(b) > 0
a < b	a.compareTo(b) < 0
a >= b	a.compareTo(b) >= 0
a <= b	a.compareTo(b) <= 0

How to do it...

1. Declare the `Position` data class with x, y, z properties related to the current position in the Cartesian coordinates system:

```
data class Position(val x: Float, val y: Float, val z: Float)
```

2. Add a `plus` operator implementation for the `Position` class:

```
data class Position(val x: Float, val y: Float, val z: Float) {
    operator fun plus(other: Position) =
        Position(x + other.x, y + other.y, z + other.z)
}
```

3. Overload the `minus` operator:

```
data class Position(val x: Float, val y: Float, val z: Float) {
    operator fun plus(other: Position) =
        Position(x + other.x, y + other.y, z + other.z)

    operator fun minus(other: Position) =
        Position(x - other.x, y - other.y, z - other.z)
}
```

How it works...

Now we can use the `Position` class together with `plus` and `minus` operators. Let's try using the minus operator:

```
val position1 = Position(132.5f, 4f, 3.43f)
val position2 = position1 - Position(1.5f, 400f, 11.56f)
print(position2)
```

That's it. The preceding code is going to print the following result to the console:

```
Position(x=131.0, y=-396.0, z=-8.13)
```

There's more...

Some of the operators have their corresponding compound *assign* operators defined. Once we have overloaded the plus and minus operators, we can use the plusAssign (+=) and minusAssign (-=) operators automatically. For example, we can use the plusAssign operator to update the Position instance state as follows:

```
var position = Position(132.5f, 4f, 3.5f)
position += Position(1f, 1f, 1f)
print(position)
```

As a result, we will get the position variable with the following state:

```
Position(x=133.5, y=5.0, z=4.5)
```

It is important to note that the *assign* operator returns the Unit. This makes it a better choice than an original basic operator (for example, plus or minus) in terms of memory allocations efficiency when updating an instance. In contrast, the base operators are returning new instances every time.

It is good to know that Kotlin offers operators overloading for Java classes as well. To overload the operator, we just need to add a proper method to the class that has the name of the operator and the public visibility modifier. Here is what the Java version of the Position class with the overloaded plus operator would look like:

```
public class Position {
        private final float x;
        private final float y;
        private final float z;
        public Position(float x, float y, float z) {
            this.x = x;
            this.y = y;
            this.z = z;
        }
        public int getX() {
            return x;
        }
        public int getY() {
            return y;
        }
        public float getZ() {
            return z;
        }
```

```
    public Position plus(Position pos) {
        return new Position(pos.getX() + x, pos.getY() + y,
        pos.getZ() + z);
    }
}
```

And here is how it could be used in Kotlin code:

```
val position = Position(2.f, 9.f, 55.5f) += (2.f, 2.f, 2.f)
```

The Kotlin standard library also contains predefined implementations of different operators. One that you should use on a daily basis is the plus operator for a MutableCollection type. This allows for adding new elements to the collection in the following way:

```
val list = mutableListOf("A", "B", "C")
list += "D"
print(list)
```

As a result, the preceding code will print the following output to the console:

```
[A, B, C, D]
```

Shaping Code with Kotlin Functional Programming Features

3

In this chapter, we will cover the following recipes:

- Working effectively with lambda expressions
- Discovering basic scoping functions – `let`, `also`, and `apply`
- Initializing objects the clean way using the `run` scoping function
- Working with higher-order functions
- Functions currying
- Function composition
- Implementing the Either Monad design pattern
- Approach to automatic function memoization

Introduction

Despite the fact that Kotlin is recognized implicitly as an object-oriented language, it is still open to other programming styles and paradigms. Thanks to Kotlin's built-in features, we are able to apply functional programming patterns to our code with ease. Having the possibility to return functions from other functions or to pass a function as a parameter allows us to benefit from a deferred computation. In addition, we are able to return functions, instead of already-computed values, on different layers in the code. This results in the lazy-evaluation feature.

Compared to Scala or other functional programming languages, Kotlin doesn't require us to use dedicated, functional style design patterns. It also lacks some of their out-of-the-box implementations. However, in return, it brings more flexibility to developers as far as software architecture and implementation details are concerned. The Kotlin language and standard library components provide full built-in support for basic functional programming concepts. And more sophisticated ones can always be implemented from scratch or reused from some of the available external libraries. The ones worth giving a try are the Kotlin Arrow (`http://arrow-kt.io`) and funKTionale (`https://github.com/MarioAriasC/funKTionale`) projects. However, keep in mind the words of Robert C. Martin—*It is perfectly possible to write a program that is both object-oriented and functional. Not only is it possible, it is desirable. There is no "OO vs FP," the two are orthogonal and coexist nicely.* It should be understood that functional programming is only one available tool. It should be used wisely and only where it is applicable.

This chapter focuses on explaining functional programming features supported by Kotlin internally. It gives you hands-on experience in solving real-life problems by using state-of-the-art functional programming concepts. By the end of the chapter, you should be familiar with the Kotlin language support for the functional programming approach and standard library components that can help implement it.

Working effectively with lambda expressions

In this recipe, we are going to explore the concept of lambdas and closures. We are going to write part of an Android application code responsible for handling button-click actions.

Getting ready

In order to implement this recipe's code, you need to create a new Android application project using Android Studio IDE.

Let's assume we have the following class, which is a sort of a controller of the application view layer:

```
class RegistrationScreen : Activity() {
    private val submitButton: Button by lazy {
findViewById(R.id.submit_button)  }

    override fun onCreate(savedInstanceState: Bundle?) {
```

```
        // hook function called once the screen is displayed
    }
}
```

It contains a reference to the `submitButton: Button` instance. Inside the `onCreate()` function we are going to implement logic responsible for handling the button clicks. Once the button is clicked, we want to make it invisible.

In order to invoke some action when the button is clicked, we need to call the `View.setOnClickListener(listener: OnClickListener)` function on the `View` subclass. The `OnClickListener` is a functional interface defined as follows:

```
public interface OnClickListener {
    void onClick(View view);
}
```

Under the hood, the Android OS invokes the `onClick()` function when the user clicks the view.

There are two ways of implementing a functional interface in Kotlin:

- Defining an object that implements the interface:

```
val myInterfaceInstance = object: MyInterface {
    override fun foo() {
        // foo function body
    }
}
```

- Treating the interface as a function and implementing it, for example, in the form of the lambda:

```
val myInterfaceAsFunction: () -> Unit = {
    // foo function body
}
```

How to do it...

1. Call the `setOnClickListener` function and pass an empty `OnClickListener` instance as a lambda expression:

```
class RegistrationScreen : Activity() {
    private val submitButton: Button by lazy {
findViewById(R.id.submit_button) }
```

```
        override fun onCreate(savedInstanceState: Bundle?) {
            submitButton.setOnClickListener { view: View ->
                // do something on click
            }
        }
    }
```

2. Modify the visibility of the `submitButton` instance inside the function body:

```
class RegistrationScreen : Activity() {
    private val submitButton: Button by lazy {
findViewById(R.id.submit_button) }

        override fun onCreate(savedInstanceState: Bundle?) {
            submitButton.setOnClickListener {
                submitButton.visibility = View.INVISIBLE
            }
        }
    }
```

How it works...

Thanks to treating `OnClickListener` as a function, we were able to implement it in the clean and concise form of a lambda expression. The lambda's body will globally be invoked whenever the user clicks the button. In our case, once the button is clicked, it will be hidden away.

Lambda expressions are one of the most essential functional features of the language and are used extensively in the standard library components. They can be seen as an abbreviated form of a function or a functional interface implementation. Lambdas help to organize code correctly and reduce a lot of boilerplate code. The syntax of a lambda expression can be seen as a block of code placed between { } symbols. Lambda expressions can have function arguments defined explicitly, for example:

```
val myFunction: (View) -> Unit = { view ->
    view.visibility = View.INVISIBLE
}
```

For the sake of brevity, the explicit parameter can be omitted. However, we can still access it using `it` modifier:

```
val myFunction: (View) -> Unit = {
    it.visibility = View.INVISIBLE
}
```

There's more...

When working with lambdas, whenever we want to execute the code inside their body, we need to call the `invoke()` function on them or its equivalent, the `()` operator:

```
val callback: () -> Unit = { println("The job is done!") }
callback.invoke()
callback()
```

The preceding code is going to print the text twice:

```
"The job is done!"
"The job is done!"
```

There is also another clean way of passing functions as the parameters to other functions. We can do it using function references:

```
fun hideView(view: View): Unit  {
    view.visibility = View.INVISIBLE
}

submitButton.setOnClickListener(::hideView)
```

The function references approach can be particularly useful for reusing the function implementation across the codebase.

Discovering basic scoping functions – let, also, apply

In this recipe, we are going to explore three useful extension functions from the standard library—let, `also`, and `apply`. They work great together with lambda expressions and help to write clean and safe code. We are going to practice their usage while applying them to implement a sequence of data-processing operations.

Getting ready

Let's assume we can fetch the date using the following function:

```
fun getPlayers(): List<Player>?
```

Here, the `Player` class is defined like this:

```
data class Player(val name: String, val bestScore: Int)
```

We would like to perform the following sequence of operations to the `getPlayers()` function result:

1. Print the original set of players in the list to the console
2. Sort the collection of the `Player` objects in descending order
3. Transform collection `Player` objects into the list of strings obtained from the `Player.name` property
4. Limit the collection to the first element and print it to the console

In order to accomplish the task, first, we need to get familiar with the characteristics of the `let`, `also`, and `apply` functions. They are provided in the standard library as extension functions for a generic type. Let's explore the headers of the `let`, `also`, and `apply` functions:

```
public inline fun <T, R> T.let(block: (T) -> R): R

public inline fun <T> T.also(block: (T) -> Unit): T

public inline fun <T> T.apply(block: T.() -> Unit): T
```

They look similar, however, there are some subtle differences in return types and in parameters. The following table compares the three functions:

Function	Return type	Argument in block argument	Block argument definition
`let`	R (from block body)	Explicit it	`(T) -> R`
`also`	T (this)	Explicit it	`(T) -> Unit`
`apply`	T (this)	Implicit this	`T.() -> Unit`

How to do it...

1. Use the `let` function together with the safe operator to assure null safety:

   ```
   getPlayers()?.let {}
   ```

2. Inside the `let` function's lambda parameter block, use the `also()` function to print the original set of players in the list to the console:

   ```
   getPlayers()?.let {
       it.also {
   ```

```
            println("${it.size} players records fetched")
            println(it)
        }
    }
```

3. Use the `let()` function to perform sorting and mapping transformations:

```
getPlayers()?.let {
    it.also {
        println("${it.size} players records fetched")
        println(it)
    }.let {
        it.sortedByDescending { it.bestScore }
    }
}
```

4. Limit the collection of players to a single `Player` instance with the highest score using the `let()` function:

```
getPlayers()?.let {
    it.also {
        println("${it.size} players records fetched")
        println(it)
    }.let {
        it.sortedByDescending { it.bestScore }
    }.let {
        it.first()
    }
}
```

5. Print the name of the best player to the console:

```
getPlayers()?.let {
    it.also {
        println("${it.size} players records fetched")
        println(it)
    }.let {
        it.sortedByDescending { it.bestScore }
    }.let {
        it.first()
    }.apply {
        val name = this.name
        print("Best Player: $name")
    }
}
```

How it works...

Let's test our implementation. For the sake of the test, we can assume that the getPlayers() function returns the following results:

```
fun getPlayers(): List<Player>? = listOf(
        Player("Stefan Madej", 109),
        Player("Adam Ondra", 323),
        Player("Chris Charma", 239))
```

The code we have implemented is going to print the following output to the console:

```
3 players records fetched
[Player(name=Stefan Madej, bestScore=109), Player(name=Adam Ondra,
bestScore=323), Player(name=Chris Charma, bestScore=239)]
Best Player: Adam Ondra
```

Note that, in the case of the apply() function, we can omit this keyword while accessing class properties and functions inside the function lambda block:

```
apply {
    print("Best Player: $name")
}
```

It was just used in the example code for the sake of clarity.

The useful feature of the let() function is that it can be used to assure the null safety of the given object. In the following example inside the let scope, the players argument will always hold a not null value even if some background thread tries to modify the original value of the mutable results variable:

```
var result: List<Player>? = getPlayers()
result?.let { players: List<Player> ->
    ...
}
```

See also

- If you'd like to learn more about lambda expressions, check out the *Working effectively with lambda expressions* recipe

Initializing objects the clean way using the run scoping function

In this recipe, we are going to explore another useful extension function provided by the standard library, called `run()`. We are going to use it in order to create and set up an instance of the `java.util.Calendar` class.

Getting ready

First, let's explore the characteristics of the `run()` function defined in the standard library with the following function header:

```
public inline fun <T, R> T.run(block: T.() -> R): R
```

It is declared as an extension function for a generic type. The `run` function provides implicit `this` parameter inside the `block` argument and returns the result of the `block` execution.

How to do it...

1. Declare an instance of the `Calendar.Builder` class and apply the `run()` function to it:

   ```
   val calendar = Calendar.Builder().run {
       build()
   }
   ```

2. Add the desired properties to the builder:

   ```
   val calendar = Calendar.Builder().run {
       setCalendarType("iso8601")
       setDate(2018, 1, 18)
       setTimeZone(TimeZone.getTimeZone("GMT-8:00"))
       build()
   }
   ```

3. Print the date from the calendar to the console:

   ```
   val calendar = Calendar.Builder().run {
       setCalendarType("iso8601")
       setDate(2018, 1, 18)
   ```

```
        setTimeZone(TimeZone.getTimeZone("GMT-8:00"))
        build()
    }
    print(calendar.time)
```

How it works...

The `run` function is applied to the `Calendar.Builder` instance. Inside the lambda passed to the `run` function, we can access the `Calendar.Builder` properties and methods via `this` modifier. In other words, inside the `run` function block, we are accessing the scope of the `Calendar.Builder` instance. In the recipe code, we are omitting to invoke `Builder` methods with `this` keyword. We can call them directly because the `run` function allows accessing the `Builder` instance inside its scope by an implicit `this` modifier.

There's more...

We can also use the `run()` function together with the safe `?` operator to provide null safety of the object referenced by `this` keyword inside the `run()` function scope. You can see it in action in the following example of configuring the Android `WebView` class:

```
webview.settings?.run {
    this.javaScriptEnabled = true
    this.domStorageEnabled = false
}
```

In the preceding piece of code, we are ensuring that the `settings` property is not null inside the `run` function scope and we can access it with `this` keyword.

See also

- The Kotlin standard library offers another similar extension function, called `apply()`, which is useful for the initialization of objects. The main difference is that it returns an original instance of the object it was called on. You can explore it in the *Implementing builders the smart way* recipe in Chapter 5, *Tasteful Design Patterns Adopting Kotlin Concepts*.

Working with higher-order functions

Kotlin is designed to provide first-class support for operating on functions. For example, we are able to easily pass functions as parameters to a function. We can also create a function that can return another function. This kind of a function is called a *higher-order function*. This powerful feature helps to write a functional style code easily. The possibility to return a function instead of a value makes along with the ability to pass a function instance to an other function as an argument, makes it possible to defer computations and to shape code cleanly. In this recipe, we are going to implement a helper function that is going to measure the execution time of other functions passed to it as an argument.

How to do it...

Implement the measureTime function:

```kotlin
fun measureTime(block: () -> Unit): Long {
    val start = System.currentTimeMillis()
    block()
    val end = System.currentTimeMillis()
    return end - start
}
```

How it works...

The measureTime() function takes an argument, called block, of the functional type. The block function parameter is invoked inside the measureTime() function using the () modifier. Finally, the difference between timestamps (before and after the block execution) is returned.

Let's analyze the following example showing the measureTime() function in action. We can consider having the following function responsible for computing the factorial of a given integer:

```kotlin
fun factorial(n: Int): Long {
    sleep(10)
    return if (n == 1) n.toLong() else n * factorial(n - 1)
}
```

In order to measure the `factorial()` function execution time we can use the `measureTime()` function as follows:

```
val duration = measureTime {
    factorial(13)
}
print("$duration ms")
```

As the result, we get the execution time printed to the console:

154 ms

Note that it is also possible to pass a function reference instead of a lambda instance as the parameter to the `measureTime()` function:

```
fun foo() = sleep(1000)
val duration = measureTime(::foo)
print("$duration ms")
```

Functions currying

Currying is a common technique in functional programming. It allows transforming a given function that takes multiple arguments into a sequence of functions, each having a single argument. Each of the resulting functions handles one argument of the original (uncurried) function and returns another function.

In this recipe, we are going to implement an automatic currying mechanism that could be applied to any function taking three parameters.

Getting ready

To understand the concept of function currying, let's consider the following example of a function handling three parameters:

```
fun foo(a: A, b: B, c: C): D
```

Its curried form would look like this:

```
fun carriedFoo(a: A): (B) -> (C) -> D
```

In other words, the curried form of the `foo` function would take a single argument of the `A` type and return another function of the following type: `(B) -> (C) -> D`. The returned function is responsible for handling the second argument of the original function and returns another function, which takes the third argument and returns a value of type `D`.

In the next section, we are going to implement the `curried()` extension function for the generic functional type declared as follows: `<P1, P2, P3, R> ((P1, P2, P3)`. The `curried()` function is going to return a chain of single-argument functions and will be applicable to any function which takes three arguments.

How to do it...

1. Declare a header of the `curried()` function:

   ```
   fun <P1, P2, P3, R> ((P1, P2, P3) -> R).curried(): (P1) -> (P2) ->
   (P3) -> R
   ```

2. Implement the `curried()` function body:

   ```
   fun <P1, P2, P3, R> ((P1, P2, P3) -> R).curried(): (P1) -> (P2) ->
   (P3) -> R =
           { p1: P1 ->
               { p2: P2 ->
                   { p3: P3 ->
                       this(p1, p2, p3)
                   }
               }
           }
   ```

How it works...

Let's explore how to use the `curried()` function in action. In the following example we are going to call `curried()` on the following function instance which is responsible for computing a sum of three integers:

```
fun sum(a: Int, b: Int, c: Int): Int = a + b + c
```

In order to obtain a curried form of the `sum()` function, we have to invoke the `curried()` function on its reference:

```
::sum.curried()
```

Then we can invoke the curried sum function in the following way:

```
val result: Int = ::sum.curried() (1) (2) (3)
```

In the end, the `result` variable is going to be assigned an integer value equal to 6.

 In order to invoke the `curried()` extension function, we access the `sum()` function reference using the `::` modifier. Then we invoke the next functions from the function sequence returned by the curried function one by one.

The preceding code could be written in an equivalent more verbose form with explicit types declarations:

```
val sum3: (a: Int) -> (b: Int) -> (c: Int) -> Int = ::sum.curried()
val sum2: (b: Int) -> (c: Int) -> Int = sum3(1)
val sum1: (c: Int) -> Int = sum2(2)
val result: Int = sum1(3)
```

Under the hood, the currying mechanism implementation is just returning functions nested inside each other. Every time the specific function is invoked, it returns another function with the arity reduced by one.

There's more...

There is a similar pattern called *partial application.* It is more flexible than currying as it doesn't limit the number of arguments handled by each of the functions. For example, given a `foo` function declared as follows:

```
fun foo(a: A, b: B, c: C): D
```

We could transform it into the following form:

```
fun foo(a: A, c: C) -> (B) -> D
```

Both currying and partial application are useful whenever we can't provide the full number of required arguments to the function in the current scope. We can apply only the available ones to the function and return the transformed function.

Function composition

In the *Functions currying* recipe, we discovered a neat way of transforming a function to extract new functions from it. In this recipe, we are going to work on implementing the opposite transformation. It would be useful to have the option to merge a number of existing functions' declarations and define a new function from them. This is a common functional programming pattern called *functions composition*. Kotlin doesn't provide function composition mechanism out of the box. However, thanks to the extended built-in support for operations on functional types, we are able to implement a reusable mechanism for the composition manually.

Getting ready

In order to get familiar with function composition, let's study the following example. Let's say we have the following functions defined:

```
fun length(word: String) = word.length
fun isEven(x:Int): Boolean = x.rem(2) == 0
```

The first one is responsible for returning the length of a given string. The second one checks whether a given integer is even. In order to define a new function based on those two functions, we can make nested function calls:

```
fun isCharCountEven(word: String): Boolean = isEven(length(word))
```

This works fine, however, it would be useful if we were able to operate on the function references instead. In order to make it more concise we'd like to be able to declare the isCharCountEven() function using the following syntax for the functions composition:

```
val isCharCountEven: (word: String) -> Boolean = ::length and ::isEven
```

How to do it...

1. Declare an infix extension function for the single-argument function called and():

```
infix fun <P1, R, R2> ((P1) -> R).and(function: (R) -> R2): (P1) ->
R2 = {

}
```

2. Invoke the base function and the one passed as an argument of and() internally:

```
infix fun <P1, R, R2> ((P1) -> R).and(function: (R) -> R2): (P1) ->
R2 = {
    function(this(it))
}
```

How it works...

In order to explore our function composition implementation, let's use the and() function to compose the isCharCountEven() function using the length() property and the isEven() function:

```
fun length(word: String) = word.length
fun isEven(x:Int): Boolean = x.rem(2) == 0
val isCharCountEven: (word: String) -> Boolean = ::length and ::isEven
print(isCharCountEven("pneumonoultramicroscopicsilicovolcanoconiosis"))
```

The preceding code is going to return the following output:

false

Under the hood, the and() extension function just invokes the given two functions one inside another. However, thanks to the infix notation we can perform the composition in the code while avoiding nested function calls. Moreover, the result of the ::length and ::isEven call in the preceding example returns a new function instance which can be easily reused, just like a normal function.

Implementing the Either Monad design pattern

The concept of Monad is one of the fundamental functional programming design patterns. We can understand a Monad as an encapsulation for a data type that adds a specific functionality to it or provides custom handlers for different states of the encapsulated object. One of the most commonly used is a Maybe monad. The Maybe monad is supposed to provide information about the enclosed property presence. It can return an instance of the wrapped type whenever it's available or nothing when it's not. Java 8 introduced the Optional<T> class, which is implementing the Maybe concept. It's a great way to avoid operating on null values.

However, apart from having the information about the unavailable state, we would often like to be able to provide some additional information. For example, if the server returns an empty response, it would be useful to get an error code or a message instead of the `null` or an empty response string. This is a scenario for another type of Monad, usually called `Either`, which we are going to implement in this recipe.

How to do it...

1. Declare `Either` as a `sealed` class:

    ```
    sealed class Either<out E, out V>
    ```

2. Add two subclasses of `Either`, representing Error and Value:

    ```
    sealed class Either<out L, out R> {
        data class Left<out L>(val left: L) : Either<L, Nothing>()
        data class Right<out R>(val right: R) : Either<Nothing, R>()
    }
    ```

3. Add factory functions for the convenient instantiating of `Either`:

    ```
    sealed class Either<out L, out R> {
        data class Left<out L>(val left: L) : Either<L, Nothing>()
        data class Right<out R>(val right: R) : Either<Nothing, R>()

        companion object {
            fun <R> right(value: R): Either<Nothing, R> =
            Either.Right(value)
            fun <L> left(value: L): Either<L, Nothing> =
            Either.Left(value)
        }
    }
    ```

How it works...

In order to make use of the class `Either` and benefit from the `Either.right()` and `Either.left()` methods, we can implement a `getEither()` function that will try to perform some operation passed to it as a parameter. If the operation succeeds, it is going to return the `Either.Right` instance holding the result of the operation, otherwise, it is going to return `Either.Left`, holding a thrown exception instance:

```
fun <V> getEither(action: () -> V): Either<Exception, V> =
        try { Either.right(action()) } catch (e: Exception) {
```

```
Either.left(e) }
```

By convention, we use the `Either.Right` type to provide a default value and `Either.Left` to handle any possible edge cases.

There's more...

One of the essential functional programming features the `Either` Monad can provide, is the ability to apply functions to its values. We can simply extend the `Either` class with the `fold()` function, which can take two functions as the parameters. The first function that should be applied to the `Either.Left` type and second, that should be applied to `Either.Right`:

```
sealed class Either<out L, out R> {
    data class Left<out L>(val left: L) : Either<L, Nothing>()
    data class Right<out R>(val right: R) : Either<Nothing, R>()

    fun <T> fold(leftOp: (L) -> T, rightOp: (R) -> T): T = when (this) {
        is Left -> leftOp(this.left)
        is Right -> rightOp(this.right)
    }

    //...
}
```

The `fold()` function is going to return a value from either the `leftOp` or `rightOp` function, whichever is used. We can illustrate the usage of the `fold()` function with a server-request parsing example.

Let's say we have the following types declared:

```
data class Response(val json: JsonObject)
data class ErrorResponse(val code: Int, val message: String)
```

We also have a function responsible for delivering a backend response:

```
fun someGetRequest(): Either<ErrorResponse, Response> = //..
```

We can use the `fold()` function to handle the returned value in the right way:

```
someGetRequest().fold({
    showErrorInfo(it.message)
}, {
    parseAndDisplayResults(it.json)
})
```

We could also extend the `Either` class with other useful functions similar to the ones available in the standard library for data-processing operations—map, `filter`, and `exists`.

Approach to automatic functions memoization

Memoization is a technique used to optimize the program-execution speed by caching the results of expensive function calls and reusing their ready values when they are required again. Although memoization causes an obvious trade-off between memory usage and computation time, often it's crucial to provide the desired performance. Usually, we apply this pattern to computationally-expensive functions. It can help to optimize recursive functions that call themselves multiple times with the same parameters' values. Memoization can easily be added internally to function implementation. However, in this recipe, we are going to create a general-purpose, reusable memoization mechanism that could be applied to any function.

How to do it...

1. Declare a `Memoizer` class responsible for caching the results:

```
class Memoizer<P, R> private constructor() {

    private val map = ConcurrentHashMap<P, R>()

    private fun doMemoize(function: (P) -> R):
        (P) -> R = { param: P ->
        map.computeIfAbsent(param) { param: P ->
                function(param)
            }
        }

    companion object {
        fun <T, U> memoize(function: (T) -> U): (T) -> U =
                Memoizer<T, U>().doMemoize(function)
    }
}
```

2. Provide a `memoized()` extension function for the `(P) -> R` function type:

```
fun <P, R> ((P) -> R).memoized(): (P) -> R = Memoizer.memoize<P,
R>(this)
```

How it works...

The `memoize()` function takes an instance of a one-argument function as its argument. The `Memoizer` class contains the `ConcurrentHashmap<P, R>` instance, which is used to cache the function's return values. The map stores functions passed to `memoize()` as arguments as the keys, and it puts their return values as its values. First, the `memoize()` function looks up the value for a specific param of the function passed as an argument. If the value is present in the map, it is returned. Otherwise, the function is executed and its result is both returned by `memoize()` and put into the map. This is achieved using the handy `inline fun <K, V> ConcurrentMap<K, V>.computeIfAbsent(key: K, defaultValue: () -> V): V` extension function provided by the standard library.

Additionally, we provide an extension function `memoized()` for the `Function1` type that allows us to apply the `memoize()` function directly to the function references.

 Under the hood functions in Kotlin are compiled to the `FunctionN` interface instances in the Java bytecode, where `N` corresponds to the number of function arguments. Thanks to that fact, we are able to declare an extension function for a function. For example, in order to add an extension function for the function taking two arguments, `(P, Q) -> R`, we need to define an extension as `fun <P, Q, R> Function2<P, Q, R>.myExtension(): MyReturnType`.

Now, let's take a look at how we could benefit from the `memoized()` function in action. Let's consider a function that computes the factorial of an integer recursively:

```
fun factorial(n: Int): Long = if (n == 1) n.toLong() else n * factorial(n -
1)
```

We can apply the `memoized()` extension function to enable results-caching:

```
val cachedFactorial = ::factorial.memoized()
println(" Execution time: " + measureNanoTime { cachedFactorial(12) } + "
ns")
println(" Execution time: " + measureNanoTime { cachedFactorial(13) } + "
ns")
```

The preceding code gives the following output on a standard computer:

```
Execution time: 1547274 ns
Execution time: 24690 ns
```

As you can see, even though the second computation requires a higher number of recursive calls of the `factorial()` function, it takes much less time than the first computation.

There's more...

We could implement similar automatic memoization implementations for the other functions that take more than one argument. In order to declare an extension function for a function taking N arguments, we'd have to implement an extension function for the `FunctionN` type.

4
Powerful Data Processing

In this chapter, we will cover the following recipes:

- Composing and consuming collections the easy way
- Filtering datasets
- Automatic `null` removal
- Sorting data with custom comparators
- Building strings based on dataset elements
- Dividing data into subsets
- Transforming data with `map` and `flatMap`
- Folding and reducing datasets
- Grouping data

Introduction

This chapter focuses on exploring standard library support for declarative-style operations on collections. The following recipes present solutions to different types of programming problem related to dataset transformations, reductions, and grouping. We will learn how to approach data processing operations with a functional programming style, together with the powerful data-processing extensions built into the standard library.

Composing and consuming collections the easy way

The Kotlin standard library provides a number of handy extensions that make collections creation and merging easy and safe. We are going to learn them step by step. Let's assume we have the following `Message` class defined:

```
data class Message(val text: String,
                   val sender: String,
                   val timestamp: Instant = Instant.now())
```

In this recipe, we are going to create two sample collections containing `Message` instances and merge them into one list of `Message` objects. Next, we are going to iterate through the list of messages and print their text to the console.

Getting ready

Kotlin standard library provides two basic interfaces which represent collection data structure—`Collection` and `MutableCollection`, both extending the `Iterable` interface. The first one defines an immutable collection that only supports read access to its elements. The second interface allows us to both add and remove elements. There are also more specialized interfaces that extend the `Collection` and `MutableCollection` base types, such as `List`, `MutableList`, `Set`, and `MutableSet`.

There are many functions available for creating collections of different types. The most commonly used ones are the `<T> listOf(vararg elements: T)` function, which instantiates a `List` instance, and `<T> mutableListOf(vararg elements: T)`, which returns an instance of `MutableList` for the elements given as a function's arguments.

How to do it...

1. Let's declare two lists containing sample data:

```
val sentMessages = listOf (
    Message("Hi Agat, any plans for the evening?", "Samuel"),
    Message("Great, I'll take some wine too", "Samuel")
)
val inboxMessages = mutableListOf(
        Message("Let's go out of town and watch the stars
tonight!",
```

```
            "Agat"),
        Message("Excelent!", "Agat")
    )
```

2. Merge `sentMessages` and `inboxMessages` into one collection:

```
val allMessages: List<Message> = sentMessages + inboxMessages
```

3. Print out the text of the `Message` objects stored in the `allMessages` list to the console:

```
val allMessages: List<Message> = sentMessages + inboxMessages
allMessages.forEach { (text, _) ->
    println(text)
}
```

How it works...

As the result, our code is going to print the following text to the console:

```
Hi Agat, any plans for the evening?
Great, I'll take some wine too
Let's go out of town and watch the stars tonight!
Excelent!
```

In order to add elements of one collection to another, we are using the + operator. The standard library overloads this operator with the code responsible for merging elements of two `Collection` type instances collections into one instance. The `sentMessages` and `inboxMessages` variables are declared as `List` instances. The `plus` function returns a new `Collection` instance, containing elements of the `sentMessages` and `inboxMessages` lists. Finally, we use the `forEach()` function to iterate through the next elements of the list. In the lambda block passed to the `forEach` function, we are print the `text` property of the current `Message` to the console. We are destructuring the lambda's argument of the `Message` type and accessing its text property directly inside the `println()` function.

There's more...

The standard library also overloads a – operator for the Collection type. We could use it to subtract some elements from the collection. For example, we could use it like this:

```
val receivedMessages = allMessages - sentMessages
receivedMessages.forEach { (text, _) ->
```

```
    println(text)
}
```

And we would get the following output:

```
Let's go out of town and watch the stars tonight!
Excelent!
```

We could also use the standard `for` loop to implement the iteration:

```
for (msg in allMessages) {
    println(msg.text)
}
```

See also

- You can learn more about destructuring declarations in the *Destructuring types* recipe in `Chapter 2`, *Expressive Functions and Adjustable Interfaces*
- If you'd like to master lambda expressions, you can take a look at the *Working effectively with lambdas and closures* recipe from `Chapter 3`, *Shaping Code with Kotlin Functional Programming Features*

Filtering datasets

Filtering is one of the most common programming challenges in the data processing field. In this recipe, we are going to explore the standard library's built-in extension functions that provide an easy way to filter the `Iterable` data types. Let's assume we have the following `Message` class declaration:

```
data class Message(val text: String,
                   val sender: String,
                   val receiver: String,
                   val folder: Folder = Folder.INBOX,
                   val timestamp: Instant = Instant.now())

enum class Folder { INBOX, SENT }
```

The `getMessages()` function returns the following data:

```
fun getMessages() = mutableListOf(
        Message("Je t'aime", "Agat", "Sam", Folder.INBOX),
        Message("Hey, Let's go climbing tomorrow", "Stefan", "Sam",
Folder.INBOX),
```

```
            Message("<3", "Sam", "Agat", Folder.SENT),
            Message("Yeah!", "Sam", "Stefan", Folder.SENT)
    )
```

We are going to apply a filtering operation to the getMessages() function that will return only the messages with the Folder.INBOX property and with the sender property equal to Agat.

Getting ready

To implement the filtering transformation, we are going to use the Iterable<T>.filter(predicate: (T) -> Boolean) extension function provided by the standard library. The filter() function takes a predicate function that returns true or false values for the given element of the generic Iterable dataset type T.

How to do it...

1. Apply filtering to the getMessages() function:

   ```
   getMessages().filter { it.folder == Folder.INBOX && it.sender ==
   "Agat" }
   ```

2. Iterate through the filtered messages and print their messages to the console:

   ```
   getMessages().filter { it.folder == Folder.INBOX && it.sender ==
   "Agat" }
    .forEach { (text) ->
        println(text)
    }
   ```

How it works...

We are applying the filter function to the results of the getMessages() function. We pass a lambda block to the filter function, which returns a Boolean for each of the list's elements. The filter function returns a list containing filtered objects. Finally, we use the forEach() function to iterate through the next elements of the list. In the lambda block passed to the forEach function, we print the text property of the current Message to the console.

As a result, the code from the preceding section is going to print the following output to the console:

```
Je t'aime
```

There's more...

The Kotlin standard library offers corresponding `filter()` extension functions for other types, such as `Array`, `Sequence`, and `Map`. There are also many variations of the filter function that can be useful for specific scenarios. You can find all of them in the official documentation of the Kotlin standard library `kotlin.collections` package at `http://kotlinlang.org/api/latest/jvm/stdlib/kotlin.collections`.

See also

- If you'd like to master lambda expressions, you can take a look at the *Working effectively with lambdas and closures* recipe from `Chapter 3`, *Shaping Code with Kotlin Functional Programming Features*

Automatic null removal

While working with poorly designed APIs of servers or external libraries, we often need to deal with receiving null return values. Thankfully, there are a number of standard library features that allow us to handle null values effectively. In this recipe, we are going to implement a data preprocessing operation which will remove all the nulls from the dataset automatically. Let's say we are working with an external API that provides us with the latest news feed. Unfortunately, it's not null-safe and can return random null values. For example, let's assume we have a `getNews(): List<News>` function that returns the following data:

```
fun getNews() = listOf(
  News("Kotlin 1.2.40 is out!", "https://blog.jetbrains.com/kotlin/"),
  News("Google launches Android KTX Kotlin extensions for developers",
  "https://android-developers.googleblog.com/"),
  null,
  null,
  News("How to Pick a Career", "waitbutwhy.com")
)
```

The News class is defined as follows:

```
data class News(val title: String, val url: String)
```

How to do it...

Apply the filterNotNull function to the getNews() function:

```
getNews()
        .filterNotNull()
        .forEachIndexed { index, news ->
            println("$index. $news")
        }
```

How it works...

As a result, we are going to get the following output printed to the console:

```
0. News(title=Kotlin 1.2.40 is out!,
url=https://blog.jetbrains.com/kotlin/)
1. News(title=Google launches Android KTX Kotlin extensions for developers,
url=https://android-developers.googleblog.com/)
2. News(title=How to Pick a Career, url=waitbutwhy.com)
```

In contrast, the code without the filterNotNull() function is as follows:

```
getNews().forEachIndexed { index, news ->
    println("$index. ${news.toString()}")
}
```

This will print the following output to the console:

```
0. News(title=Kotlin 1.2.40 is out!,
url=https://blog.jetbrains.com/kotlin/)
1. News(title=Google launches Android KTX Kotlin extensions for developers,
url=https://android-developers.googleblog.com/)
2. null
3. null
4. News(title=How to Pick a Career, url=waitbutwhy.com)
```

The `Iterable.filterNotNull()` extension function removes all the null values from the original dataset. Under the hood, it copies non-null values to a newly created `List` instance. That's why it is more efficient to use sequences instead of collections in order to provide lazy evaluation for large datasets.

See also

- In the *Filtering data sets* recipe, we explored how to use the basic `filter()` function form provided by the standard library
- If you'd like to master lambda expressions, you can take a look at the *Working effectively with lambdas and closures* recipe from Chapter 3, *Shaping Code with Kotlin Functional Programming Features*

Sorting data with custom comparators

In this recipe, we are going to explore the support for sorting collections' elements by their properties.

Getting started

Let's assume we are dealing with the two collections of the `Message` type declared as follows:

```
data class Message(val text: String,
                   val sender: String,
                   val receiver: String,
                   val time: Instant = Instant.now())
```

These are provided by the `allMessages` variable:

```
val sentMessages = listOf(
        Message("I'm programming in Kotlin, of course",
                "Samuel",
                "Agat",
                Instant.parse("2018-12-18T10:13:35Z")),
        Message("Sure!",
                "Samuel",
                "Agat",
                Instant.parse("2018-12-18T10:15:35Z"))
```

```
    )
val inboxMessages = mutableListOf(
        Message("Hey Sam, any plans for the evening?",
                "Samuel",
                "Agat",
                Instant.parse("2018-12-18T10:12:35Z")),
        Message("That's cool, can I join you?",
                "Samuel",
                "Agat",
                Instant.parse("2018-12-18T10:14:35Z"))
    )
val allMessages = sentMessages + inboxMessages
```

If we print the text of consecutive messages from the `allMessages` list, we get the following text printed to the console:

```
I'm learning Kotlin, of course
Sure!
Hey Sam, any plans for the evening?
That's cool, can I join you?
```

That doesn't look right. The messages should be displayed in chronological order. That means they should be sorted by the `time` property.

How to do it...

1. Apply the `sortedBy` function to the `allMessages` collection:

   ```
   allMessages.sortedBy { it.time }
   ```

2. Print the sorted elements to the console:

   ```
   allMessages.sortedBy { it.time }
           .forEach {
               println(it.text)
           }
   ```

How it works...

If we run the preceding code, we get the following output:

```
I'm programming in Kotlin, of course
Sure!
```

```
Hey Sam, any plans for the evening?
That's cool, can I join you?
```

Now, all the messages are sorted properly and the conversation makes sense.

There's more...

If our collection consisted of objects that implement the Comparable interface, we would be able to sort it simply by applying a `sorted()` function to it. The Kotlin standard library also provides more specialized versions of the `sortedBy()` function, such as `sortedByDescending()` and `sortedWith()`. The first one works as a base-sorting function, but it returns the dataset sorted with the opposite order. The `sortedWith()` function allows us to sort the list with a custom comparator. For example, to sort a collection of the `Message` type elements first by `sender` and next by the `time` property, we could write the following code:

```
allMessages.sortedWith(compareBy({it.sender}, {it.time}))
```

Building strings based on dataset elements

Sometimes, we all face the problem of generating text based on collections' elements. This is where the `Iterable.joinToString()` extension function can help. For example, we can consider working on an email-message-forwarding feature. When a user clicks the forward button, the original message's body text is concatenated, with the prefix looking something like this:

```
<br/>
<p>---------- Forwarded message ----------</p>
<p>
From: johny.b@gmail.com <br/>
Date: 14/04/2000 <br/>
Subject: Any plans for the evening?<br/>
To: natasha@gmail.com, barbra@gmail.com<br/>
</p>
```

In this recipe, we are going to implement a function that is going to generate the recipients' string, for example:

```
To: natasha@gmail.com, barbra@gmail.com</br>
```

For a given list of `Address` type objects, it is defined as follows:

```
data class Address(val emailAddress: String, val displayName: String)
```

How to do it...

1. Declare the `generateRecipientsString()` function header:

    ```
    fun generateRecipientsString(recipients: List<Address?>): String
    ```

2. Start by removing all the `null` items from the `recipient` parameter:

    ```
    fun generateRecipientsString(recipients: List<Address?>): String =
            recipients.filterNotNull()
    ```

3. Transform collection elements of the `Address` type to the `String` type elements corresponding to the `Address.emailAddress` property:

    ```
    fun generateRecipientsString(recipients: List<Address?>): String =
            recipients.filterNotNull()
                    .map { it.emailAddress }
    ```

4. Apply the `joinToString()` function in order to merge collection elements into the string:

    ```
    fun generateRecipientsString(recipients: List<Address?>): String =
            recipients.filterNotNull()
                    .map { it.emailAddress }
                    .joinToString(", ", "To: ", "<br/>")
    ```

How it works...

The `generateRecipientsString()` function uses the `Iterable.joinToString()` extension function from the standard library `kotlin.collections` package to generate the output string. The `joinToString()` function takes three parameters—the separator character, which is used to concatenate the next substrings, the prefix, and the suffix strings. It is invoked on a collection of String values. We are also applying the preprocessing operations that are responsible for removing the `null` values from the list of the `Address` objects and mapping the `Address` type to the `String` corresponding to the `Address.emailAddress` property.

There's more...

We could also use another version of the `joinToString()` function to simplify the logic of our `generateRecipientsString()` function implementation:

```
fun generateRecipientsString(recipients: List<Address?>): String =
        recipients.filterNotNull()
            .joinToString(", ", "To: ", "<br/>") { it.emailAddress }
```

As you can see, it takes the additional argument in the form of an inlined lambda block, which acts as a transformation function that is being applied to each of the `recipients` collection elements.

See also

- To explore dataset mapping operations in more depth, you can read the *Data transformation with the map and flatMap recipe*

Dividing data into subsets

A common data-processing task is to divide a collection of data into subsets. In this recipe, we are going to explore standard library functions that allow us to buffer a collection into smaller chunks. Let's say we have a list containing a large number of `Message` type objects and we would like to transform it into collections of sub-lists of a constant size. For example, the transformation would take the original collection of *n* elements:

```
[mssg_1, mssg_2, mssg_3, mssg_4, mssg_5, mssg_6, mssg_7, ..., mssg_n]
```

And it would then split it into a collection of four element subsets:

```
[[mssg_1, mssg_2, mssg_3, mssg_4], ..., [mssg_n-3, mssg_n-2, mssg_n-1,
mssg_n]]
```

Getting ready

Let's start by declaring the `Message` class that we are going to use in the following recipe:

```
data class Message(val text: String,
                   val time: Instant = Instant.now())
```

Let's declare the `messages` variable that stores the sample data:

```
val messages = listOf(
        Message("Any plans for the evening?"),
        Message("Learning Kotlin, of course"),
        Message("I'm going to watch the new Star Wars movie"),
        Message("Would u like to join?"),
        Message("Meh, I don't know"),
        Message("See you later!"),
        Message("I like ketchup"),
        Message("Did you send CFP for Kotlin Conf?"),
        Message("Sure!")
)
```

How to do it...

1. Apply the `windowed()` function to the `messages` list:

   ```
   val pagedMessages = messages.windowed(4, partialWindows = true,
   step = 4)
   ```

2. Add a `transform: (List<T>) -> R` transformation function as an additional, inline parameter to the windowed function:

   ```
   val pagedMessages = messages.windowed(4, partialWindows = true,
   step = 4) {
       it.map { it.text }
   }
   ```

How it works...

The `windowed` function splits the original list of messages into sublists of a specified size. As a result, we get the `List<List<Message>>` type assigned to the `pagedMessages` handle. We could print the next message subsets with the following code:

```
pagedMessages.forEach { println(it) }
```

As the result, we get the following output printed to the console:

```
[Any plans for the evening?, Learning Kotlin, of course, I'm going to watch
the new Star Wars movie, Would u like to join?]
[Meh, I don't know, See you later!, I like the ketchup, Did you send CFP
for Kotlin Conf?]
[Sure!]
```

The `windowed` function takes four parameters—the size of the window, a flag saying whether partial windows should be created, a step value, and an optional transforming function that is responsible for converting each of the generated windows. In our scenario, we are using a window size equal to 4. This is why we need to specify the step value as equal to 4 as well because we want to have consecutive `Message` instances stored in the next windows. We also set the `partialWindows` argument to `true`, otherwise, the last window containing a single message would be omitted. The last param of the `windowed` function allows us to map each of the windows into another type. We are mapping each of sublists returned by the `windowed()` function into the `List<String>` type. There is also another version of the `windowed` function, without the last mapping parameter, so it can be treated as the optional one.

There's more...

There is also a handy wrapper of the `windowed()` function provided, called `chunked()`. It doesn't require the step argument and sets it automatically to the window size value. It would be a good fit for this recipe's problem, however, the `windowed()` function was explained as it's more basic.

See also

- There are other functions available that solve different list and collection division scenarios, such as the `subList()` (`https://kotlinlang.org/api/latest/jvm/stdlib/kotlin.collections/-list/sub-list.html`) and `partition()` (`https://kotlinlang.org/api/latest/jvm/stdlib/kotlin.collections/partition.html`) functions. You can find out more about them in official docs using the provided links.

Data transformation with map and flatMap

The support for declarative data mapping operations is one of the basic and most powerful features in the functional data-processing domain. Often, when working with data, we need to transform a collection of a specific type into another type. It's also a common scenario to generate a list of objects from each element of a collection and to merge all of those new objects in a target collection together. Those are the use cases where the `map()` and `flatMap()` extension functions help.

In this recipe, we are going to use both of them to implement a mapping data transformation. Let's imagine we are working on the part of the system responsible for managing university department lectures. We are given the following types:

```
class Course(val name: String, val lecturer: Lecturer, val isPaid: Boolean
= false)
class Student(val name: String, val courses: List<Course>)
class Lecturer(val name: String)
```

We also have a `getStudents(): List<Student>` function, which returns a list of all students from the database. We want to implement the `getLecturesOfCoursesWithSubscribedStudents()` function, which is going to to transform the `getStudents()` result to compute a list of lecturers whose courses are subscribed to by at least one student.

How to do it...

1. Declare a function header:

   ```
   fun getLecturesOfCoursesWithSubscribedStudents()
   ```

2. Apply the `flatMap` operation to the list of students:

   ```
   fun getLecturesOfCoursesWithSubscribedStudents() =
           getStudents()
                   .flatMap { student ->
                       student.courses
                   }
   ```

3. Limit the collections' elements to distinct values:

   ```
   fun getLecturesOfCoursesWithSubscribedStudents() =
           getStudents()
                   .flatMap { student ->
                       student.courses
                   }
                   .distinct()
   ```

4. Map the collection of the `Course` type elements to their corresponding `Lecturer` type properties:

```
fun getLecturesOfCoursesWithSubscribedStudents() =
    getStudents()
    .flatMap { student ->
        student.courses
    }
    .distinct()
    .map { course -> course.lecturer }
    .distinct()
```

How it works...

With the following `flatMap` operation, the
`getLecturesOfCoursesWithSubscribedStudents()` function is transforms the
collection of the `Student` type objects into the collection of the `Course` type by merging
elements of the `Student.courses: Collection<Course>` property:

```
getStudents()
        .flatMap { student: Student ->
            student.courses
        }
```

As the result, the preceding code returns the `Collection<Course>` type. The collection
returned by the `flatMap` operation contains a set of all the courses all of the students
(obtained from the `getStudents()` function) are subscribed to.

Next, in order to remove duplicated courses, we append the chain of operations with the
`distinct()` function. Then, we use the `map()` function. It is responsible for transforming
every single element of the `Course` type into its corresponding `Lecturer` type from the
`Course.lecturer` property. Finally, we are applying the `distinct()` function once again
to return the list of lecturers with no duplicates.

There's more...

The `map()` and `flatMap()` extension functions are also available for the `Map` data structure
type. They are useful when it comes to converting a map to a list of objects transformed
from the map's key-value pairs.

Folding and reducing data sets

While the `map()` operator takes a list of a given size and returns another list of the same size and of the modified type, the `fold()` and `reduce()` operations applied to the data set return a single element, composed of the consecutive elements of the data set. This may sound like a simple scenario for using a plain, imperative-style loop and local accumulator variable that holds a current state and is updated at each iteration. We can consider the simple task of summing up integer values. Let's consider that we want to compute a sum of consecutive integers from 0 to 10. We could achieve it using a simple `for` loop:

```
var sum = 0
(1..10).forEach {
    sum += it
}
```

However, there is an alternative, functional way of performing such computations, using the `fold()` function:

```
val sum = (1..3).toList().fold(0) { acc, i -> acc + i }
```

The second approach is desirable whenever we implement a chain of functional data-processing operations. Compared to the for loop, the `fold` function doesn't enforce consuming the collection elements explicitly and can be easily used together with other functional operators.

In this recipe, we are going make use of the `fold` function when implementing the function responsible for processing the audio album tracks. Let's assume we are given the following data types:

```
data class Track(val title: String, val durationInSeconds: Int)
data class Album(val name: String, val tracks: List<Track>)
```

and the sample `Album` class instance:

```
val album = Album("Sunny side up", listOf(
        Track("10/10", 176),
        Track("Coming Up Easy", 292),
        Track("Growing Up Beside You", 191),
        Track("Candy", 303),
        Track("Tricks of the Trade", 151)
))
```

We want to implement an extension function for the `Album` type that will return a relative start time for the `Track` given as an argument. For example, the start time of the `Growing Up Beside You` track should be 468 seconds.

How to do it...

1. Declare an extension function for the `Album` class:

```
fun Album.getStartTime(track: Track): Int
```

2. Compute the start time for the given `Track` argument:

```
fun Album.getStartTime(track: Track): Int {
    val index = tracks.indexOf(track)
    return this.tracks
            .take(index)
            .map { (name, duration) -> duration }
            .fold(0) { acc, i -> acc + i }
}
```

3. Add a safety check for the `track` argument:

```
fun Album.getStartTime(track: Track): Int {
    if (track !in tracks) throw IllegalArgumentException("Bad
    track")

    val index = tracks.indexOf(track)
    return tracks
        .take(index)
        .map { (name, duration) -> duration }
        .fold(0) { acc, i -> acc + i }
}
```

How it works...

At the very beginning, our function does a safety check for the `track` argument passed to it to verify whether it belongs to the current `Album` instance. If the given track is not found within the `Album.tracks` collection, the `IllegalArgumentException` exception is thrown. Next, we create a sublist from the `tracks` property elements containing only the elements from the 0 index to the index of the `track` passed as the function parameter. This sublist is created using the `take()` operator. Then, we map each of the `Track` type elements to the `Int` type corresponding to the duration of the track. Finally, we apply the `fold` function, to sum the `durationInSeconds` property values of the consecutive `Track` elements. The `fold` function takes the `initial` argument responsible for initializing the internal `accumulator` variable holding the current state of the folding result.

In our case, we pass 0 as the `initial` value, which corresponds to the album start time. In the second argument passed to the `fold` function, we are defining how the `accumulator` should be updated with each of the consecutive `durationInSeconds` values.

Let's test the `Album.getStartTime()` function in action:

```
println(album.getStartTime(Track("Growing Up Beside You", 191)))
println(album.getStartTime(Track("Coming Up Easy", 292)))
```

The preceding code returns the following output:

```
468
176
```

There's more...

The standard library provides a similar function, named `reduce()`, which does the same operation as `fold`. The difference between the two is that `fold` takes an explicit initial value, whereas `reduce` uses the first element from the list as the initial value.

Grouping data

The Kotlin standard library provides built-in support for the dataset *group by* operation. In this recipe, we are going to explore how to use it.

Let's assume we are working with the following types:

```
class Course(val name: String, val lecturer: Lecturer, val isPaid: Boolean
= false)
class Student(val name: String, val courses: List<Course>)
class Lecturer(val name: String)
```

We also have a `getStudents(): List<Student>` function that returns a list of all the students from the database.

Given the `getStudents(): List<Student>` function, we are going to implement the `getCoursesWithSubscribedStudents(): Map<Course, List<Student>>` function responsible for extracting the map of all the courses students are subscribed to, and the list of students subscribed to each of the courses.

How to do it...

1. Declare a function header:

```
fun getCoursesWithSubscribedStudents(): Map<Course, List<Student>>
```

2. Map each of the students to the list of the course-student pairs:

```
fun getCoursesWithSubscribedStudents(): Map<Course,
List<Student>> =
    getStudents()
            .flatMap { student ->
                student.courses.map { course -> course to student }
            }
```

3. Group the course-student pairs by `Course`:

```
fun getCoursesWithSubscribedStudents(): Map<Course,
List<Student>> =
    getStudents()
            .flatMap { student ->
                student.courses.map { course -> course to student }
            }
            .groupBy { (course, student) -> course }
```

4. Apply a mapping transformation to the `Pair<Course, List<Student>>` type:

```
fun getCoursesWithSubscribedStudents(): Map<Course,
List<Student>> =
    getStudents()
            .flatMap { student ->
                student.courses.map { course -> course to student }
            }
            .groupBy { (course, _) -> course }
            .map { (course, courseStudentPairs) ->
                course to courseStudentPairs.map { (_, student) ->
                student }
            }
```

5. Apply a `toMap()` function at the end:

```
fun getCoursesWithSubscribedStudents(): Map<Course,
List<Student>> =
    getStudents()
            .flatMap { student ->
                student.courses.map { course -> course to student }
            }
            .groupBy { (course, _) -> course }
```

```
        .map { (course, courseStudentPairs) ->
            course to courseStudentPairs.map { (_, student) ->
            student }
    }
    .toMap()
```

How it works...

We start by transforming the list of students to list of the `Pair<Course, Student>` type with the `flatMap()` function. Next, we apply the `groupBy()` function to group those pairs by a distinct `Course` instance. As the result of the grouping operation, we receive data of the following type—`Map.Entry<Course, List<Pair<Course, Student>>>`. We need to convert the `Map.Entry.value` property type to the `List<Student>` type. We achieve it with the following mapping transforming function:

```
map { (course, courseStudentPairs) ->
    course to courseStudentPairs.map { (_, student) -> student }
}
```

As a result, each `Course` instance is associated with a list of students subscribed to it (`Pair<Course, List<Student>>`). Note that the infix `to` function is being used to instantiate the Pair type. Finally, we invoke the `toMap()` function, which produces the final `Map<Course, List<Students>>` instance from the list of course-student pairs.

There's more...

We can also modify our map building operation to a more concise form by using the `mapValues` function:

```
fun getCoursesWithSubscribedStudents(): Map<Course, List<Student>> =
    getStudents()
        .flatMap { student ->
            student.courses.map { course -> course to student }
        }
        .groupBy { (course, _) -> course }
        .mapValues { (course, courseStudentPairs) ->
            courseStudentPairs.map { it -> it.second }
        }
```

See also

- The code in this recipe uses destructuring types declarations in mapping operations. If you'd like to learn more about this, you can take a look at the *Destructuring types* recipe from `Chapter 2`, *Expressive Functions and Adjustable Interfaces*.

5
Tasteful Design Patterns Adopting Kotlin Concepts

In this chapter, we will cover the following recipes:

- Implementing the Strategy pattern
- Exploring the power of the Delegation pattern
- Implementing delegated class properties
- Tracking state with the Observer pattern
- Restricting property updates with the Vetoable delegate
- Implementing the advanced Observer pattern by defining a custom property delegate
- Working with the Lazy delegate
- Implementing builders the smart way

Introduction

The following chapter is going to present popular, general-purpose design patterns applicable to a range of programming problems. The following recipes focus on exploiting Kotlin's built-in language support for implementing specific concepts and patterns. Apart from basic design patterns, such as Strategy or Builder, the chapter will focus on different usages of Delegation in a diverse set of applications and scenarios. Once you get familiar with the concepts presented in this chapter, you will be able to utilize the language's built-in features while designing and developing elegant and reliable systems.

Implementing the Strategy pattern

The Strategy design pattern is used to provide an interchangeable set of strategies that can be applied to a given input and return an output of a specific type. We can understand the concept of a strategy as an action or an algorithm that can be applied to the input. A mechanism responsible for processing input should be able to switch between provided strategies at runtime. To illustrate the Strategy pattern, we are going to implement a text-formatting mechanism that allows us to apply a transformation to the input text and print it to the console. We are going to implement a class called `Printer`, which will provide a `printText(text: String)` function for printing the text to the console. Before printing out the text to the console, the `Printer` class will perform a transformation of the given `text` parameter according to the selected text formatting strategy.

How to do it...

1. Implement the `Printer` class:

```
class Printer(val textFormattingStrategy: (String) -> String) {
    fun printText(text: String) {
        val processedText = textFormattingStrategy(text)
        println(processedText)
    }
}
```

2. Add sample strategies:

```
val lowerCaseFormattingStrategy: (String) -> String = {
    it.toLowerCase()
}

val upperCaseFormattingStrategy: (String) -> String = {
    it.toUpperCase()
}
```

How it works...

Let's start by testing how our `Printer` class works in action. First, declare two instances of the `Printer` class—the first one with the `lowerCaseFormattingStrategy` for the `textFormattingStrategy` property, and the second one with `upperCaseFormattingStrategy`:

```
val lowerCasePrinter = Printer(lowerCaseFormattingStrategy)
val upperCasePrinter = Printer(upperCaseFormattingStrategy)
```

Next, let's use them to format and display the following text:

```
val text = "This functional-style Strategy pattern looks tasty!"

lowerCasePrinter.printText(text)
upperCasePrinter.printText(text)
```

The following output will print to the console:

```
this functional-style strategy pattern looks tasty!
THIS FUNCTIONAL-STYLE STRATEGY PATTERN LOOKS TASTY!
```

The `Printer.textFormattingStrategy` property is a function that takes a single `String` argument and returns a `String` type as the output. It is invoked inside the `printText(text: String)` function with the `text` parameter, and its output is returned by the function.

There's more...

You can practice by implementing your own text-formatting strategies. Try to implement a new text formatting strategy, called `capitalizeFormattingStrategy`, that will be responsible for capitalizing the first letter of the input text. Once you're done, create a new strategy be composed of the two implemented earlier—`lowerCaseFormattingStrategy` and `capitalizeFormattingStrategy`. You can refer to the *Function composition* recipe in Chapter 3, *Shaping Code with Kotlin Functional Programming Features* to learn more about the generic way of composing functions together.

See also

- If you are not familiar with the concept of higher-order functions used to declare the `Printer.textFormattingStrategy` property, you can explore the *Working with higher-order functions* recipe from `Chapter 3`, *Shaping Code with Kotlin Functional Programming Features*

Exploring the power of the Delegation pattern

The Delegation pattern is a great alternative to typical inheritance of classes. Delegation allows a certain class to be derived from another one or to implement an interface. However, under the hood, the derived class is not a subclass of the base class but the composition is used instead to provide the properties of the base class to the derived one. Whenever a request to the properties of the base class part is made, it is being redirected to a delegated object. This is comparable to subclasses deferring a request to parent classes. However, delegation not only allows us to achieve the same code reusability as inheritance does, it's also much more powerful and customizable. Kotlin makes the Delegation pattern even more impressive because it provides a built-in support for declaring delegates using the `by` keyword.

In this recipe, we are going to implement a combination of dependent classes modeling a simple book library system. We are going to write a code of a given UML class diagram that describes a set of dependent classes using inheritance. However, we are going to use the delegation pattern instead of any inheritance occurrences.

Getting ready

We are going to work on implementing a set of the following classes using the Delegate pattern instead of inheritance:

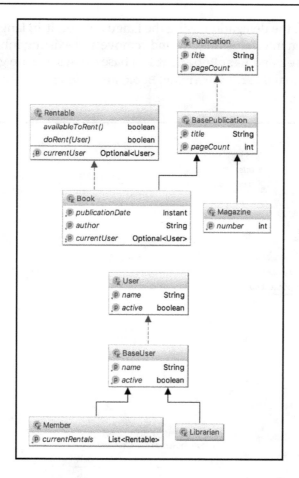

In this class diagram, you can see two base classes that are being derived from the
BasePublication class with its Book and Magazine subclasses, and the BaseUser class,
which is extended by the Member and Librarian subclasses. Note that those base classes
are implementing corresponding interfaces declaring their properties. The BaseUser class
implements the User interface, and the BasePublication class implements
the Publication interface. There is also the Rental interface, which declares methods
implemented by the Book subclass.

In order to implement the delegation using the language's built-in language features, we are going to operate on interfaces directly and remove any existing inheritance. Instead of extending the `BaseUser` and `BasePublication` base classes, we are going to use them as the properties of the final `User`, `Librarian`, `Book`, and `Magazine` classes, as presented in the following diagram:

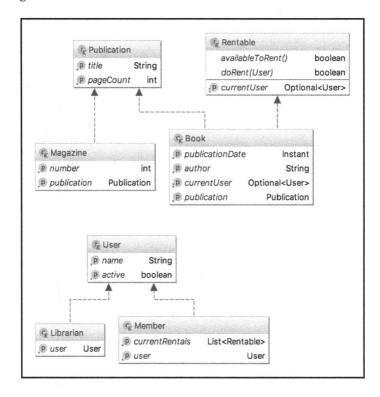

How to do it...

1. Declare the `Magazine` class implementing the `Publication` interface:

```
class Magazine(val number: Int,
               title: String,
               pageCount: Int) : Publication
```

2. Delegate the `Publication` interface to the class property of the `Publication` type:

```
class Magazine(val number: Int,
               val publication: Publication) :
        Publication by publication
```

3. Implement the `Rentable` interface:

```
interface Rentable {
    var currentUser: Optional<User>

    fun availableToRent() = !currentUser.isPresent

    fun doRent(user: User): Boolean {
        return if (availableToRent()) {
            currentUser = Optional.of(user)
            true
        } else {
            false
        }
    }
}
```

4. Implement the `Book` class, delegating its `Publication` interface functionality to the class member:

```
class Book(val publicationDate: Instant,
           val author: String,
           val publication: Publication) :
        Publication by publication, Rentable {

    override var currentUser: Optional<User> = Optional.empty()
}
```

5. Implement the `Member` and `Librarian` classes, implementing the `User` interface and delegating it to their class properties:

```
class Member(val currentRentals: List<Rentable>,
             name: String,
             isActive: Boolean,
             user: User) : User by user

class Librarian(user: User) : User by user
```

How it works...

Using the `by` keyword, we have delegated the implementation of the `User` and `Publication` interfaces to specialized objects defined as class members. In the case of the `Book` and `Magazine` classes, the responsibilities for the `Publication` interface were delegated to the `publication: Publication` class properties, and, in the case of the `Member` and `Librarian` classes, the responsibilities for the `User` interface were delegated to the `user: User` properties.

Now, let's explore how we can work with delegated types. Let's start by creating an instance of the `Book` class. We provide a `Book.publication` property of the `Publication` type by reusing the original `BasePublication` class declaration:

```
class BasePublication(override val title: String,
                      override val pageCount: Int): Publication
```

Note that we are able to access all the public members of the `Publication` interface directly from the `Book` class instance. Any requests to those `Publication` interface properties are being redirected to the `val publication` property of the `Book` class:

```
val book = Book(Instant.now(), "Sam",
        BasePublication("Kotlin Standard Library Cookbook",
          Integer.MAX_VALUE))

println("${book.title} written by ${book.author} has ${book.pageCount}
pages.")
```

In the result, the preceding code should print the following output to the console:

```
Kotlin Standard Library Cookbook written by Sam has 2147483647 pages.
```

See also

- Another great type of Delegation design pattern is related to delegating class properties. You can find out more in the *Implementing delegated class properties* recipe.

Implementing delegated class properties

Class properties in Kotlin are more than just plain class fields. The key characteristic of Kotlin properties is the fact that their values are specified by accessor functions automatically. Each class property in Kotlin has a dedicated set of accessor functions available out of the box. By default, the Kotlin compiler generates a field storing the value of the property and its getters or setters as well. Each immutable `val` property has a corresponding `get()` function provided and the mutable one declared with `var` keyword has the `set()` function in addition to a `get()` as well. We are also able to override a default implementation of the accessor function, which makes a property highly customizable and powerful. For example, we can override the `get()` function of the property and provide a custom implementation for it, which can stop the compiler from storing the value of the property in a field. Moreover, the fact that properties are represented by their accessor functions and not by the fields values makes *property delegation* possible. The basic use cases for the property delegation include:

- Implementing lazy properties—providing the value that gets computed only upon first access
- Observable properties—listeners get notified about changes to the property
- Storing properties in a map, instead of a separate field for each property

In this recipe, we are going to learn how to create a function allowing us to easily serialize class instance into JSON format by to delegating its properties to be stored in a map.

Getting ready

Similar to the interface delegation, the class property delegation is achieved using the `by` keyword in the following manner:

```
class MyClass {
    var property: String by MyDelegate
}
```

The object which is delegated to should implement one of the following interfaces—`ReadWriteProperty` or `ReadOnlyProperty` from the `kotlin.properties` package. Those interfaces expose the `getValue()` and `setValue()` functions, which provide values for the property.

We are going to use the `Gson` library to convert objects into their JSON format representation. It's a widely used Java library for working with JSON-formatted objects. You can learn more about the library on its GitHub site (`https://github.com/google/gson`). If you're using the Gradle build tool, you need to add the Gson artifact to the project dependencies:

```
dependencies {
    implementation 'com.google.code.gson:gson:2.8.4'
}
```

How to do it...

1. Implement the `Client` class containing a data property of a `Map<String, Any>` type:

   ```
   data class Client(private val data: Map<String, Any>)
   ```

2. Implement the `CreditCard` class:

   ```
   data class CreditCard(val holderName: String,
                         val number: String,
                         val cvcCode: String,
                         val expiration: Long)
   ```

3. Add the `name`, `email`, and `creditCards` properties to the `Client` class and delegate them to the `data` property:

   ```
   data class Client(private val data: Map<String, Any>) {
       val name: String by data
       val email: String by data
       val creditCards: List<CreditCard> by data
   }
   ```

4. Implement the `toJson(): String` member function, allowing us to serialize a `Client` type object into JSON format, and the `fromJson(json: String): Client` utility function responsible for the opposite operation:

   ```
   data class Client(private val data: Map<String, Any>) {
       val name: String by data
       val email: String by data
       val creditCards: List<CreditCard> by data

       /**
        * Function for serializing instance of Client class into
   ```

```
    JSON format
 */
fun toJson(): String = gson.toJson(data)

companion object {
    private val gson = Gson()

    /**
     * Utility function for instantiating Client class from
       JSON string
     */
    fun fromJson(json: String): Client {
        val mapType = object : TypeToken<Map<String,
         Any>>() {}.type
        val data: Map<String, Any> = gson.fromJson(json,
         mapType)
        return Client(data)
    }
}
}
```

How it works...

Class properties can be delegated to a `Map` or `MutableMap` instance, which contains keys of the `String` type and values of the `Any` type. The map's keys correspond to the names of the class properties and the map's values associated with them store the properties values. The map that is delegated to is being updated dynamically whenever the delegated property is updated.

Let's take a look at how we can make use of the `Client` class implemented in this recipe. We can instantiate the `Client` class by passing the `Map` instance to the class constructor:

```
val SAMPLE_CLIENT_MAP = mapOf("name" to "Mark Zuck",
        "email" to "mark@fb.com",
        "creditCards" to listOf(
                CreditCard("Mark Zuckerberg", "123345456789", "123",
                  1527330705017),
                CreditCard("Mark Zuckerberg", "987654321", "321",
                  1527330719816))
)
val client1 = Client(SAMPLE_CLIENT_MAP)
```

We can also instantiate the `Client` class using the `fromJson()` function, passing a string containing a JSON representation of the sample `Client` type object:

```
@Language("JSON")
const val SAMPLE_CLIENT_JSON =
        "{\n  \"name\": \"Mark Zuck\",
        \n  \"email\": \"mark@fb.com\",
        \n  \"creditCards\": [
        \n    {
        \n        \"holderName\": \"Mark Zuckerber\",
        \n        \"number\": \"123345456789\",
        \n        \"cvc\": \"123\",
        \n        \"expiration\": 1527330705017
        \n    },
        \n    {
        \n        \"holderName\": \"Mark Zuckerber\",
        \n        \"number\": \"987654321\",
        \n        \"cvc\": \"321\",
        \n        \"expiration\": 1527330719816
        \n    }
        \n  ]
        \n}"
val client2 = Client.fromJson(SAMPLE_CLIENT_JSON)
```

If you are working with IntelliJ IDE, you can use a cool *Language injection* feature that allows us to inject another language's code snippet as a String type and provides support for the language-specific syntax for editing and formatting. You can use it to inject JSON snippets as a Kotlin String. You can learn more about it at the official JetBrains tutorial (`https://www.jetbrains.com/help/idea/using-language-injections.html`).

Under the hood, the `Client.fromJson()` function uses Gson to convert JSON data to the `Map<String, Any>` instance.

We can now test those two ways and print the contents of both the `client1` and `client2` objects to the console:

```
println("name: ${client1.name}, mail: ${client1.email}, cards:
${client1.creditCards}")
println("name: ${client2.name}, email: ${client2.email}, cards:
${client2.creditCards}")
```

As the result, we are going to get the following output printed to the console:

```
name: Mark Zuck, email: mark@fb.com, cards: [{holderName=Mark Zuckerber,
number=123345456789, cvc=123, expiration=1.527330705017E12},
{holderName=Mark Zuckerber, number=987654321, cvc=321,
expiration=1.527330719816E12}]

name: Mark Zuck, email: mark@fb.com, cards: [CreditCard(holderName=Mark
Zuckerberg, number=123345456789, cvcCode=123, expiration=1527330705017),
CreditCard(holderName=Mark Zuckerberg, number=987654321, cvcCode=321,
expiration=1527330719816)]
```

In both cases, all the class properties are stored in the `data` map object, no matter which way of instantiating the `Client` class was chosen. The delegation of the properties to the map allowed us to implement a mechanism that exports the state of the `Client` object to the map automatically. The map object was stored internally in the `Client` class, however, it could be declared anywhere else as well.

There's more...

In this recipe, we have created the `Client` class, which contains immutable `val` properties. In order to store mutable `var` properties, we can use a `MutableMap` instance instead of a read-only `Map`.

Built-in support for class properties is a powerful feature of the language. It brings awesome possibilities to shape your code in a neat way. You should definitely give it a try when working on a more complex project. For example, you can delegate the properties of your entities to be read and written directly to and from the database. There is also a group of ready-to-use delegates built into the standard library, such as the *Lazy* or *Observable* delegates. You can learn more about their application in the next recipes in this chapter. You can explore the full set of built-in delegates in the official standard library docs: `https://kotlinlang.org/api/latest/jvm/stdlib/kotlin.properties/-delegates/index.html`.

See also

- If you'd like to explore the concept of interface delegation, you can take a look at the *Exploring the power of Delegation pattern* recipe
- You should also learn about the standard property delegates provided by the standard library

Tracking state with the Observer pattern

The Observer pattern is a concept in which an object allows us to subscribe to the changes of its state and notifies a set of its observers automatically whenever there is a change of the object state. The implementation of the Observer pattern in Kotlin is pretty easy with the help of the built-in `Observable` property delegate offered by the standard library. In this recipe, we are going to implement an observable variable that will allow us to subscribe to the changes in its state. The subscribed listener should be notified immediately after any state updates. In the following example, we are going to declare the `temperature: Int` variable and subscribe to its changes.

How to do it...

1. Define an initial value for the temperature variable:

   ```
   val initialValue = 1
   ```

2. Declare the listener for the variable that will be observed:

   ```
   val initialValue = 1
   val changesListener: (KProperty<*>, Int, Int) -> Unit =
           { _, _: Int, newValue: Int -> println("Current temperature:
   $newValue") }
   ```

3. Declare the `temperature` variable, delegating its value to the `ReadWriteProperty` instance returned by the `Delegates.observable()` function:

   ```
   val initialValue = 1
   val changesListener: (KProperty<*>, Int, Int) -> Unit =
           { _, _: Int, newValue: Int -> println("Current temperature:
   $newValue") }
   var temperature: Int by Delegates.observable(initialValue,
   changesListener)
   ```

How it works...

We are delegating the `var temperature` variable to the result of the
`Delegates.observable()` function, which returns an instance of the
`ReadWriteProperty` class. That fact makes it possible to declare `temperature` as a
mutable variable. The `observe()` function takes two arguments—the initial value, and an
instance of the hook function that is going to be invoked on every change made to the
delegated variable. In our case, we are instantiating the function as the lambda block, which
is supposed to print the new `temperature` value to the console.

Let's test how our implementation is going to work. We are going to modify the value of
the temperature directly a couple of times:

```
temperature = 10
temperature = 11
temperature = 12
temperature = 30
```

As the result, we get the following output:

```
Current temperature: 10
Current temperature: 11
Current temperature: 12
Current temperature: 30
```

On each change of the temperature value, the listener function is being invoked with the
previous and new values of the property passed to its parameters.

See also

- If you'd like to explore how the property delegates are working under the hood,
  take a look at the *Implementing delegated class properties* recipe

Restricting property updates with the Vetoable delegate

In this recipe, we are going to explore the usage of the Vetoable delegate offered by the standard library. Similar to the Observable, the Vetoable tracks the changes applied to the delegated property. However, the Vetoable delegate is able to refuse to update the delegated property if a predefined update condition is not met. We are going to declare a variable of the Int type and specify the update condition, allowing us to update the variable only if the absolute value of change is greater than or equal to 10.

How to do it...

1. Let's start by defining an initial value for the temperature variable:

   ```
   val initialValue = 1
   ```

2. Define the update condition for the observed variable:

   ```
   val initialTemperature = 1
   val updateCondition: (KProperty<*>, Int, Int) -> Boolean =
           { _, oldValue: Int, newValue: Int -> Math.abs(oldValue -
   newValue) >= 10 }
   ```

3. Declare the temperature: Int variable and delegate it to the result of the Delegates.vetoable() function:

   ```
   val initialTemperature = 1
   val updateCondition: (KProperty<*>, Int, Int) -> Boolean =
           { _, oldValue: Int, newValue: Int -> Math.abs(oldValue -
   newValue) >= 10 }
   var temperature: Int by Delegates.vetoable(initialTemperature,
   updateCondition)
   ```

How it works...

We are delegating the var temperature variable to the result of the Delegates.vetoable() function, which returns an instance of the ReadWriteProperty class. That fact makes it possible to declare temperature as a mutable variable.
The vetoable() function takes two arguments—the initial value, and an instance of the hook function that is going to be invoked on every change made to the delegated variable.

That function provides the current value of the delegated variable and a candidate for the new value. As the result, the function returns the Boolean—true if the value can be updated, and false if the update condition is not met. In our case, we are instantiating the function as the lambda block in which we check whether the absolute value of change is greater than or equal to 10:

```
{ _, oldValue: Int, newValue: Int -> Math.abs(oldValue - newValue) >= 10 }
```

Let's test how our implementation is going to work. We are going to modify the value of temperature directly a couple of times with different values and verify whether the update was approved by printing the temperature state to the console:

```
temperature = 10
println("Current temperature: $temperature")

temperature = 11
println("Current temperature: $temperature")

temperature = 12
println("Current temperature: $temperature")

temperature = 30
println("Current temperature: $temperature")
```

As the result, we get the following output printed out:

```
Current temperature: 1
Current temperature: 11
Current temperature: 11
Current temperature: 30
```

As you can see, the value of temperature remains unchanged whenever we are assigning it with values that don't satisfy the specified condition.

See also

- In the next recipe, *Implementing the advanced observer using a custom property delegate*, we are going to combine together the functionalities of the Observable and Vetoable delegates by implementing our custom delegate. Read on to explore how to both filter updates of the property and implement the Observer pattern in one property delegate.

Implementing the advanced Observer pattern by defining a custom property delegate

In this recipe, we are going to implement a custom, generic property delegate combining features of the Observable and Vetoable delegates available in the standard library. In other words, we want to implement a property delegate that allows us to notify a subscribed listener about any changes made to the observed property. At the same time, we also want the delegate to allow filtering of the updates made to the delegated property. In this example, we are going to declare the `temperature: Int` variable delegated to our custom implementation of the `ObservableVetoable` delegate class. We are going to create a generic class that allows us to pass the initial value, a function responsible for filtering property updates and a function that will be invoked immediately after the change to the property is made.

How to do it...

1. Define the custom property delegate called `ObservableVetoableDelegate` as a subclass of the `ObservableProperty` class:

```
class ObservableVetoable<T>(initialValue: T,
                            val updatePrecondition: (old: T, new: T)
                            -> Boolean,
                            val updateListener: (old: T, new: T)
                            -> Unit) :
        ObservableProperty<T>(initialValue = initialValue) {

    override fun beforeChange(property: KProperty<*>,
                              oldValue: T,
                              newValue: T): Boolean =
        updatePrecondition(oldValue, newValue)

    override fun afterChange(property: KProperty<*>,
                             oldValue: T,
                             newValue: T) =
        updateListener(oldValue, newValue)
}
```

2. Define the `initialTemperature`, `updatePrecondition`, and `updateListener` arguments required by the `ObservableVetoable` class:

```
val initialTemperature = 1
val updatePrecondition: (Int, Int) -> Boolean =
        { oldValue, newValue -> Math.abs(oldValue - newValue) >= 10
}

val updateListener: (Int, Int) -> Unit = { _, newValue ->
println(newValue) }
```

3. Declare the `temperature: Int` variable by delegating it to the `ObservableVetoable` class instance:

```
var temperature: Int by ObservableVetoable(initialTemperature,
                                           updatePrecondition,
                                           updateListener)
```

How it works...

We have defined the `ObservableVetoable` class and delegated the `var temperature:` `Int` variable to the `ObservableVetoable` instance. Our `ObservableVetoable` class extends the `ObservableProperty` class, which implements the `ReadWriteProperty` interface under the hood. Thanks to this, `ObservableProperty` allows us to delegate mutable properties to it. The `ObservableProperty` class also has the `beforeChange():` `Boolean` and `afterChange(): Unit` open functions, which are being invoked inside the `setValue()` function:

```
public override fun setValue(thisRef: Any?, property: KProperty<*>, value:
T) {
    val oldValue = this.value
    if (!beforeChange(property, oldValue, value)) {
        return
    }
    this.value = value
    afterChange(property, oldValue, value)
}
```

As you can see, whenever the delegated property is assigned to a new value, the `beforeChange()` function is invoked to check whether the new value meets specified conditions. If the conditions are met, the property gets updated and the `afterChange()` function is called. In fact, our `ObservableVetoable` class takes instances of the function implementations, `updatePrecondition` and `updateListener`, which override the `beforeChange()` and `afterChange()` base functions. This way, we are able to both observe the changes made to the delegated property and notify the changes listener immediately to filter the changes being made to it.

For example, we can test our implementation by updating the `temperature` variable five times with different values:

```
temperature = 11
temperature = 12
temperature = 13
temperature = 14
temperature = 30
```

As a result, we are going to have only two lines printed to the console:

```
11
30
```

This means that our mechanism is working properly because our update precondition function is checking whether the absolute value of change is greater than or equal to `10`. `updateListener()` is called only when the new value is accepted by the `updatePrecondition()` function.

See also

- If you'd like to get familiar with the basics of property-delegation support in Kotlin, take a look at the *Implementing delegated class properties* recipe, which contains an in-depth introduction and explanation of the language support for the delegation concept
- You can also explore the *Restricting property's updates with Vetoable* delegate and the *Tracking state with Observer pattern* recipes to get familiar with the Observer and Vetoable delegates provided by the standard library

Working with the Lazy delegate

Lazy initialization is another design pattern that has its dedicated delegate implementation included in the standard library. The concept of lazy initialization refers to the strategy of delaying the creation of an object, calculation of a value, or execution of some expensive operation until the first time it's needed. In this recipe, we are going to define a sample class, `CoffeeMaker`, and declare an object of its type via the Lazy delegate. Then we are going to perform example operations on the object to explore how the lazy delegate is working in action.

How to do it...

1. Let's start with defining the `CoffeeMaker` class:

```
class CoffeeMaker {
    init {
        println("I'm being created right now... Ready to make some
          coffee!")
    }

    fun makeEspresso() {
        println("Un espresso, per favore!")
    }

    fun makeAmericano() {
        print("Un caffè americano, per favore!")
    }
}
```

2. Declare a variable of the `CoffeMaker` type using the `lazy` delegate:

```
val coffeeMaker: CoffeeMaker by lazy { CoffeeMaker() }
```

How it works...

Let's test out how the `coffeeMaker` instance is going to behave by running the following code:

```
val coffeMaker: CoffeeMaker by lazy { CoffeeMaker() }
println("Is the CoffeMaker created already?")
```

```
coffeMaker.makeEspresso()
coffeMaker.makeAmericano()
```

And here is the output printed out to the console:

```
Is the CoffeMaker created already?
I'm being created right now... Ready to make some coffe!
Un espresso, per favore!
Un caffè americano, per favore!
```

As you might have imagined, the constructor of the `CoffeeMaker` class is being called only upon the first request to the `coffeeMaker` variable. In fact, the lambda block passed to the lazy function is invoked on the call to the `coffeeMaker.makeEspresso()` function. Once the `CoffeeMaker` object is instantiated, it's reused for any consecutive operations performed on it.

 By default, the evaluation of lazy properties is synchronized; the value is computed only in one thread, and all threads will see the same value. If the synchronization of the initialization delegate is not required so that multiple threads can execute it simultaneously, pass `LazyThreadSafetyMode.PUBLICATION` as a parameter to the `lazy()` function. And if you're sure that the initialization will always happen on a single thread, you can use the `LazyThreadSafetyMode.NONE` mode, which doesn't incur any thread-safety guarantees and the related overhead (`https://kotlinlang.org/docs/reference/delegated-properties.html#lazy`).

The `lazy()` function creates and returns an instance of the `Lazy<T>` interface:

```
public interface Lazy<out T> {
    public val value: T
    public fun isInitialized(): Boolean
}
```

As you can see, the `value` property is immutable and it's not possible to declare a mutable variable or property using the lazy delegate. Under the hood, the `Lazy` implementation returns a specific value of the object it holds and is checking internally if it has been already evaluated. During the first access to the object, the `initializer` function passed to the lazy function as an argument is being executed and its result is being assigned to the dedicated property. Later, the cached value is going to be used instead of re-evaluating the value each time.

See also

- If you'd like to explore how the property delegates are working under the hood, take a look at the *Implementing delegated class properties* recipe

Implementing builders the smart way

The Builder design pattern is one of the most commonly used mechanisms for instantiating complex types in the Java language. It was strongly recommended by Joshua Bloch in the *Effective Java* book. Bloch says the builders should be used when we need to implement multiple constructors. He also mentions that builder pattern simulates named optional parameters. However, in Kotlin, those arguments for implementing a specialized builder class are no longer valid. Kotlin allows us to provide default values to the class constructor arguments and properties and it has built-in support for named arguments. Given those Kotlin features, there is no need to implement the builders in most scenarios since we can simply achieve their functionality using the language's built-in concepts. However, in Kotlin, we can adapt the Builder pattern to achieve even more. We are going to utilize the concept of the builder, together with higher-order functions and the possibility of inlining lambda parameters, to define the DSL-like syntax for instantiating instances of a given class.

Getting ready

Let's assume we have the `Dialog` class specified in some external dependency with an interface provided as follows:

```
class Dialog {
    lateinit var title: String
    lateinit var message: String
    lateinit var messageColor: String
    lateinit var image: ByteArray

    fun show() = println("Dialog...\n$this")

    override fun toString() = "Title: $title \nImage: $image \nMessage:
    $message"
}
```

The `Dialog` class exposes the following properties—`title: String`, `message: String`, `messageColor: String`, and `image: File`. We are going to implement a `DialogBuilder` class, which allows us to instantiate the `Dialog` class using the builder pattern. As the result, we would like to create a mechanism that allows us to instantiate the `Dialog` type using a DSL-like syntax similar to the JSON format:

```
val dialog: Dialog =
    dialog {
        title {
            "Title"
        }
        message {
            text = "Message"
            color = "#FF0000"
        }
        image {
            File("path")
        }
    }
```

How to do it...

1. Create the `DialogBuilder` class containing properties responsible for holding values needed by the `Dialog` class properties:

```
class DialogBuilder() {
  private var titleHolder = "-"
  private var messageHolder = StyleableText("-", "#000")
  private var imageHolder: File = File.createTempFile("empty", "")

  class StyleableText(
      var text: String = "",
      var color: String = "#000"
  )
}
```

2. Add the `title()`, `message()`, and `image()` functions, allowing us to modify the `titleHolder`, `message`, and `image` properties:

```
class DialogBuilder() {
  private var titleHolder = "-"
  private var messageHolder = StyleableText("-", "#000")
  private var imageHolder: File = File.createTempFile("empty", "")

  fun title(block: () -> String) {
```

```
        titleHolder = block()
    }

    fun message(block: StyleableText.() -> Unit) {
        messageHolder.apply { block() }
    }

    fun image(block: File.() -> Unit) {
        imageHolder.apply { block() }
    }
    class StyleableText(
        var text: String = "",
        var color: String = "#000"
    )
}
```

3. Add the `build()` function, returning the `Dialog` class instance:

```
class DialogBuilder() {
    private var titleHolder = "-"
    private var messageHolder = StyleableText("-", "#000")
    private var imageHolder: File = File.createTempFile("empty", "")

    fun title(block: () -> String) {
        titleHolder = block()
    }

    fun message(block: StyleableText.() -> Unit) {
        messageHolder.apply { block() }
    }

    fun image(block: File.() -> Unit) {
        imageHolder.apply { block() }
    }

    fun build(): Dialog = Dialog().apply {
        title = titleHolder
        message = messageHolder.text
        messageColor = messageHolder.color

        imageHolder.apply {
            image = readBytes()
        }
    }

    class StyleableText(
        var text: String = "",
        var color: String = "#000"
```

```
    )
  }
```

4. Declare a constructor taking a function responsible for initialization of the `DialogBuilder` class:

```kotlin
class DialogBuilder() {
  private var titleHolder = "-"
  private var messageHolder = StyleableText("-", "#000")
  private var imageHolder: File = File.createTempFile("empty", "")

  constructor(initBlock: DialogBuilder.() -> Unit): this() {
      initBlock()
  }

  fun title(block: () -> String) {
      titleHolder = block()
  }

  fun message(block: StyleableText.() -> Unit) {
      messageHolder.apply { block() }
  }

  fun image(block: File.() -> Unit) {
      imageHolder.apply { block() }
  }

  fun build(): Dialog = Dialog().apply {
      title = titleHolder
      message = messageHolder.text
      messageColor = messageHolder.color

      imageHolder.apply {
          image = readBytes()
      }
  }

  class StyleableText(
      var text: String = "",
      var color: String = "#000"
  )
}
```

5. Implement the `dialog()` helper function, taking a function responsible for initializing `DialogBuilder` and returning the `Dialog` class instance:

```
fun dialog(block: DialogBuilder.() -> Unit): Dialog =
DialogBuilder(block).build()
```

How it works...

Let's start by testing how we can use our `dialog()` function in action. Let's use it to define a sample `Dialog` class instance:

```
val dialog =
        dialog {
            title {
                "Warning!"
            }
            message {
                text = "You have 99999 viruses on your computer!"
                color = "#FF0000"
            }
            image {
                File.createTempFile("red_alert", "png")
            }
        }
```

Now, we can invoke the `show()` function on the `dialog` variable, which is going print the following output to the console:

```
Dialog...
Title: Warning!
Image: [B@548c4f57
Message: You have 99999 viruses on your computer!
```

That's pretty cool! The `DialogBuilder` class allows us to compose instances of the `Dialog` type in a readable and natural way.

Implementing the new syntax for the `Dialog` class composition was possible by the use of higher-order functions and inline notation for lambda arguments. Note that each of the `DialogBuilder` functions, `title()`, `message()`, and `image()`, that are preparing information about the state of the target class properties, take a single functional parameter. The functional arguments are passed in the form of lambda blocks. There are two kinds of function types being used as parameters in the builder methods—the first one, which simply returns a specific value for the property, and the second one, which returns a function with a receiver type. The second type of the function returns `Unit` but takes an instance of the receiver type.

Function types are allowed to have an additional receiver type, which is declared before the dot. In the following notation—the `A.(B) ->` `C` type represents a function that can be invoked on a receiver object of `A` type with a parameter of `B` type and return a value of `C`. Inside the body of the function literal, the receiver object passed to a call becomes an implicit `this`, so that you can access the members of that receiver object without any additional qualifiers, or access the receiver object using `this` keyword. You can read more about the available function types and their applications on the official Kotlin reference: `https://kotlinlang.` `org/docs/reference/lambdas.html#function-types`.

For example, the `title(block: () -> String)` function simply invokes the block function and assigns the result to the `DialogBuilder.titleHolder` property. On the other hand, whenever we are dealing with complex types, such as `StyleableText`, we are using the second approach using a function with a receiver type function's argument. For example, let's analyze the `message(block: StyleableText.() -> Unit)` function:

```
fun message(block: StyleableText.() -> Unit) {
    messageHolder.apply { block() }
}
```

Under the hood, it is executing the `block: StyleableText.() -> Unit` argument to modify the `messageHolder: StyleableText` property instance directly.
The `block` argument is being invoked using the `()` modifier inside the `apply` function, which in this case provides the access to the `messageHolder` instance via a local `this` keyword. The same approach is used in the constructor of the `DialogBuilder` class:

```
constructor(initBlock: DialogBuilder.() -> Unit): this() {
    initBlock()
}
```

The receiver of the `DialogBuilder` type is being provided to the functional parameter and the function passed as `initBlock` is invoked inside the constructor, allowing us to modify its state.

There's more...

The concept of DSL-style builders is used extensively in many Kotlin libraries and frameworks. It is also employed by the standard library. For example, we can use the `html` function from the `kotlinx.html` library (`https://github.com/Kotlin/kotlinx.html`) to generate the HTML code:

```
val result =
        html {
            head {
                title { +"HTML encoding with Kotlin" }
            }
            body {
                h1 { "HTML encoding with Kotlin" }
                p { +"this format can be used as an alternative to HTML" }

                // an element with attributes and text content
                a(href = "http://jetbrains.com/kotlin") { +"Kotlin" }
            }
        }
println(result)
```

The preceding code is going to generate a valid HTML code and print it to the console:

```
<html>
    <head>
        <title>HTML encoding with Kotlin</title>
    </head>
    <body>
        <h1>HTML encoding with Kotlin</h1>
        <p>this format can be used as an alternative to HTML</p>
        <a href="http://jetbrains.com/kotlin">Kotlin</a>
    </body>
</html>
```

You can explore even more awesome applications of the Builders in Kotlin at `https://kotlinlang.org/docs/reference/type-safe-builders.html`.

See also

- If you'd like to learn more about the technical details of higher-order functions and inline notation for functional parameters, you can investigate the *Inlining parameters of closure type* recipe from Chapter 2, *Expressive Functions and Adjustable Interfaces* and the *Working with higher order functions* recipe from Chapter 3, *Shaping Code with Kotlin Functional Programming Features*

Friendly I/O Operations

6

In this chapter, we will cover the following recipes:

- Reading the contents of a file
- Ensuring stream closing with the `use` function
- Reading the contents of a file line by line
- Writing the contents to a file
- Appending a file
- Easy files copying
- Traversing files in a directory

Introduction

This chapter focuses on explaining the Kotlin approach to working with JVM `File`, `InputStream`, and `OutputStream` types. We are going to explore the group of extension functions offered by the standard library under the `kotlin.io` package, which focus on enhancing support for I/O operations. Note that at the moment, with the Kotlin version 1.2, the following recipes are applicable only to code targeting the JVM platform.

Reading the contents of a file

In this recipe, we are going to retrieve the contents of a file as text and print it to the console. We are going to use the standard library `File.readText()` extension function, returning a `String` representing the text content of the given `File` instance.

Getting ready

Make sure you have a sample non-empty file included in your project to read its contents. You can clone the sample project provided with the book's GitHub repository: https://github.com/PacktPublishing/Kotlin-Standard-Library-Cookbook. In this recipe, we are going to use the file1.txt file located in the src/main/resources directory in the sample project.

How to do it...

1. Import the File.separator constant and assign an alias to it:

```
import java.io.File.separator as SEPARATOR
```

2. Declare a String storing a path to the file we are going to read:

```
val filePahtName =
"src${SEPARATOR}main${SEPARATOR}resources${SEPARATOR}file1.txt"
```

3. Instantiate a File using the specified path:

```
val filePahtName =
"src${SEPARATOR}main${SEPARATOR}resources${SEPARATOR}file1.txt"
val file = File(filePahtName)
```

4. Read the text from the file and print it to the console:

```
val filePahtName =
"src${SEPARATOR}main${SEPARATOR}resources${SEPARATOR}file1.txt"
val file = File(filePahtName)
val fileText: String = file.readText()
println(fileText)
```

How it works...

The readText() extension function is returning the String value representing the text of the given file. This is a convenient way of reading the file contents since it wraps the low-level logic of reading bytes from the FileInputStream class. Under the hood, before reading the bytes of the file, the function checks whether the file has the proper size to be stored in memory.

Keep in mind that, if the file size is too large, OutOfMemoryError is thrown. Whenever the file is too big to be processed at once, you should access its content using BufferedReader. You can easily obtain the BufferedReader instance by calling the File.bufferedReader() extension function.

The readText() function can also take the charset: Charset argument, which by default is set to the Charsets.UTF_8 value. If you'd like to use another charset, you can specify it by passing a proper one as the charset argument. You can find the available charset types inside the kotlin.text.Charsets object. You can also find them listed in the official documentation: https://kotlinlang.org/api/latest/jvm/stdlib/kotlin.text/-charsets.

You may have noticed we are using the File.separator constant instead of the hardcoded "/" char. Thanks to that, we can be sure the correct directory-separating character will be used on different platforms. For the sake of brevity, you can import File.separator with an alias, for example import java.io.File.separator as separator.

See also

- You can also check out the *Reading the contents of a file line by line* recipe, which explains how to read the text content of a file line by line effectively

Ensuring stream closing with the use function

Whenever we are accessing the contents of a File via FileInputStream or FileOutputStream, we should remember to close them once we've finished working on the file. Unclosed streams may lead to memory leaks and a significant decrease in performance. In this recipe, we are going to explore how to employ the use() extension function offered by the standard library under the kotlin.io package for automatic stream closing.

Getting ready

Make sure you have a sample non-empty file included in your project to read its contents. You can clone the sample project provided with the book's GitHub repository: `https://github.com/PacktPublishing/Kotlin-Standard-Library-Cookbook`. In this recipe, we are going to use the `file1.txt` file located in the `src/main/resources` directory in the sample project.

How to do it...

1. Import the `File.separator` constant and assign an alias to it:

   ```
   import java.io.File.separator as SEPARATOR
   ```

2. Declare a `String` storing a path to the file we are going to read:

   ```
   val filePahtName =
   "src${SEPARATOR}main${SEPARATOR}resources${SEPARATOR}file1.txt"
   ```

3. Instantiate a `FileInputStream` for the `file1.txt` file:

   ```
   val filePahtName =
   "src${SEPARATOR}main${SEPARATOR}resources${SEPARATOR}file1.txt"
   val stream = File(filePahtName).inputStream()
   ```

4. Read the bytes from the stream inside the `use()` function:

   ```
   val fileName =
   "src${SEPARATOR}main${SEPARATOR}resources${SEPARATOR}file1.txt"
   val stream = File(fileName).inputStream()
   stream.use {
       it.readBytes().also { println(String(it)) }
   }
   ```

How it works...

First, we create the `FileInputStream` instance using the `File.inputStream()` extension function. Next, we invoke the `use()` extension function on our stream instance, passing a lambda block containing operations we want to perform on the stream as the argument.

Under the hood, after invoking the lambda expression, the `use()` function calls the `close()` function on the stream variable. We can check that, when we try to access the file using the `stream` variable once again, we will get a `java.io.IOException: Stream Closed` exception thrown.

 The `use()` function extends any type that implements the `Closeable` interface. It takes a lambda block as the argument, passing an instance of the closeable resource to the lambda as the parameter. The `use` function returns the value returned by the lambda block. Under the hood, there is a `try...catch` block being used where the `close()` function of the resource is invoked inside the `finally` block.

Reading the contents of a file line by line

In this recipe, we are going to retrieve the contents of a file as a set of consecutive text lines. We are going to use the standard library extension function, `File.readLines()`, to return a `List` of a `String` type representing the next lines of the given `File` instance.

Getting ready

Make sure you have a sample non-empty file included in your project to read its contents. You can clone the sample project provided with the book at the GitHub repository: https://github.com/PacktPublishing/Kotlin-Standard-Library-Cookbook. In this recipe, we are going to use the `file1.txt` file located in the `src/main/resources` directory in the sample project.

How to do it...

1. Import the `File.separator` constant and assign an alias to it:

   ```
   import java.io.File.separator as SEPARATOR
   ```

2. Declare a `String` storing a path to the file we are going to read:

   ```
   val filePahtName =
   "src${SEPARATOR}main${SEPARATOR}resources${SEPARATOR}file1.txt"
   ```

3. Instantiate a `File` using the specified path:

```
val filePahtName =
"src${SEPARATOR}main${SEPARATOR}resources${SEPARATOR}file1.txt"
val file = File(filePahtName)
```

4. Read the text from the file and print it to the console:

```
val filePathName =
"src${SEPARATOR}main${SEPARATOR}resources${SEPARATOR}file1.txt"
val file = File(fileName)
val fileLines = file.readLines()
fileLines.forEach { println(it) }
```

How it works...

The `readLines()` extension function returns the `List<String>` instance representing the lines of text of the given file. This is a convenient way of reading the file contents since it wraps the low-level logic of reading bytes from the `FileInputStream` class.

Keep in mind that, if the file size is too large, `OutOfMemoryError` is thrown. Whenever the file is too big to be processed at once, you should access its content using `BufferedReader`. You can easily obtain the `BufferedReader` instance by calling the `File.bufferedReader()` extension function.

The `readLines()` function can also take the `charset: Charset` argument, which by default is set to the `Charsets.UTF_8` value. If you'd like to use another charset, you can specify it by passing a proper one as the `charset` argument. You can find the available charset types inside the `kotlin.text.Charsets` object. You can also find them listed in the official documentation: `https://kotlinlang.org/api/latest/jvm/stdlib/kotlin.text/-charsets`.

You may have noticed we are using the `File.separator` constant instead of the hardcoded `"/"` char. Thanks to that, we can be sure the correct directory-separating character will be used on different platforms. For the sake of brevity, you can import `File.separator` with an alias, for example `import java.io.File.separator as separator`.

See also

- You can also check out the *Reading the contents of a file* recipe, which explains how to retrieve the text contents of the file at once as the `String` value

Writing the contents to a file

In this recipe, we are going to learn how to easily create a new `File` and write text to it. We are going to use the `File.writeText()` extension function offered by the standard library. Then, we are going to verify whether the file was successfully created and whether it contains the proper contents by printing it to the console.

How to do it...

1. Import the `File.separator` constant and assign an alias to it:

   ```
   import java.io.File.separator as SEPARATOR
   ```

2. Specify the path to the new file we are going to create:

   ```
   val fileName =
   "src${SEPARATOR}main${SEPARATOR}resources${SEPARATOR}temp_file"
   ```

3. Instantiate the file using the specified file path:

   ```
   val fileName =
   "src${SEPARATOR}main${SEPARATOR}resources${SEPARATOR}temp_file"
   val file = File(fileName)
   ```

4. Write the text to the file using the `writeText()` function inside the `apply` block:

   ```
   val fileName =
   "src${SEPARATOR}main${SEPARATOR}resources${SEPARATOR}temp_file"
   val file = File(fileName)
   file.apply {
       val text =
           "\"No one in the brief history of computing " +
               "has ever written a piece of perfect software. " +
               "It's unlikely that you'll be the first.\" - Andy Hunt"
   ```

```
        writeText(text)
    }
```

5. Print the contents of `temp_file` to the console:

```
val fileName =
"src${SEPARATOR}main${SEPARATOR}resources${SEPARATOR}temp_file"
val file = File(fileName)
file.apply {
    val text =
        "\"No one in the brief history of computing " +
            "has ever written a piece of perfect software. " +
            "It's unlikely that you'll be the first.\" - Andy Hunt"
    writeText(text)
}
file.readText().apply { println(this) }
```

How it works...

As the result of executing the preceding code, a new `temp_file` file is going to be created under the `src/main/resources` directory. Keep in mind that in case the `temp_file` already exists it is going to be overridden. Next, with the help of the `writeText()` function its contents are going to be printed to the console:

> **"No one in the brief history of computing has ever written a piece of perfect software. It's unlikely that you'll be the first."** - Andy Hunt

The `writeText()` function wraps the `java.io.FileOutputStream` API, providing a neat way of writing content to the file. Under the hood, it accesses `FileOutputStream` inside the `use()` function, so you can be sure that it autocloses any streams that are opened during the write operation.

> If the text you want to write to the file is too large to be processed at once, you can use the `BufferedWriter` API to allow you to write and append the file. You can easily obtain an instance of `BufferedWriter` using the `File.bufferedWriter()` extension function.

You can also pass the additional `charset: Charset` argument to `writeText()`, which by default is equal to the `Charsets.UTF_8` value. If you'd like to use another charset, you can specify it by passing a proper one as the `charset` argument. You can find the available charset types inside the `kotlin.text.Charsets` object. You can also find them listed in the official documentation at `https://kotlinlang.org/api/latest/jvm/stdlib/kotlin.text/-charsets`.

See also

- Check out the *Appending a file* recipe to learn how to modify a file's content in a flexible way by appending it

Appending a file

In this recipe, we are going to learn how to easily create a new `File` and write text to it by appending its content a number of times. We are going to use the `File.appendText()` extension function offered by the standard library. Then, we are going to verify whether the file was successfully created and whether it contains the proper content by printing it to the console.

How to do it...

1. Import the `File.separator` constant and assign an alias to it:

   ```
   import java.io.File.separator as SEPARATOR
   ```

2. Specify the path to the new file we are going to create:

   ```
   val fileName =
   "src${SEPARATOR}main${SEPARATOR}resources${SEPARATOR}temp_file"
   ```

3. Instantiate the file using the specified file path:

   ```
   val fileName =
   "src${SEPARATOR}main${SEPARATOR}resources${SEPARATOR}temp_file"
   val file = File(fileName)
   ```

4. Delete the file if it already exists:

```
val fileName =
"src${SEPARATOR}main${SEPARATOR}resources${SEPARATOR}temp_file"
val file = File(fileName)
if (file.exists()) file.delete()
```

5. Append the file with the next String values:

```
val fileName =
"src${SEPARATOR}main${SEPARATOR}resources${SEPARATOR}temp_file"
val file = File(fileName)
if (file.exists()) file.delete()

file.apply {
    appendText("\"A language that doesn't affect the way you think
")
    appendText("about programming ")
    appendText("is worth knowing.\"")
    appendText("\n")
    appendBytes("Alan Perlis".toByteArray())
}
```

6. Print the file's contents to the console:

```
val fileName =
"src${SEPARATOR}main${SEPARATOR}resources${SEPARATOR}temp_file"
val file = File(fileName)
if (file.exists()) file.delete()

file.apply {
    appendText("\"A language that doesn't affect the way you think
")
    appendText("about programming ")
    appendText("is worth knowing.\"")
    appendText("\n")
    appendBytes("Alan Perlis".toByteArray())
}

file.readText().let { println(it) }
```

How it works...

As a result of executing the preceding code, a new `temp_file` file is going to be created under the `src/main/resources` directory, and its content is going to be printed out to the console:

```
"A language that doesn't affect the way you think about programming is worth
knowing."
Alan Perlis
```

The `appendText()` and `appendBytes()` functions wrap the `java.io.FileOutputStream` API, providing a neat way of appending content to the file. Under the hood, they access `FileOutputStream` inside the `use()` function, so you can be sure that it autocloses any streams that are opened during the write operation.

 If the text you want to write to the file is too large to be processed at once, you can use the `BufferedWriter` API, which allows you to write and append the file. You can easily obtain an instance of `BufferedWriter` using the `File.bufferedWriter()` extension function.

You can also pass the additional `charset: Charset` argument to the `appendText()` function, which by default is equal to the `Charsets.UTF_8` value. If you'd like to use another charset, you can specify it by passing a proper one as the `charset` argument. You can find the available charset types inside the `kotlin.text.Charsets` object. You can also find them listed in the official documentation at `https://kotlinlang.org/api/latest/jvm/stdlib/kotlin.text/-charsets`.

Easy file copying

In this recipe, we are going to explore a neat way of copying a file's contents into a new file. We are going to obtain a sample `File` instance from the specified path and copy its content into the new file. Finally, we are going to print the contents of both files to the console to verify the operation.

Getting ready

Make sure you have a sample non-empty file included in your project to read its contents. You can clone the sample project provided with the book at the GitHub repository: `https:/` `/github.com/PacktPublishing/Kotlin-Standard-Library-Cookbook`. In this recipe, we are going to use the `file2.txt` file located in the `src/main/resources` directory in the sample project.

How to do it...

1. Import the `File.separator` constant and assign an alias to it:

   ```
   import java.io.File.separator as SEPARATOR
   ```

2. Instantiate a `File` instance for the specified `file2.txt` path:

   ```
   val sourceFileName =
   "src${SEPARATOR}main${SEPARATOR}resources${SEPARATOR}file2.txt"
   val sourceFile = File(sourceFileName)
   ```

3. Create a new `File` called `file2_copy.txt`:

   ```
   val sourceFileName =
   "src${SEPARATOR}main${SEPARATOR}resources${SEPARATOR}file2.txt"
   val sourceFile = File(sourceFileName)

   val targetFileName =
   "src${SEPARATOR}main${SEPARATOR}resources${SEPARATOR}file2_copy.txt
   "
   val targetFile = File(targetFileName)
   ```

4. If `file2_copy.txt` exists, delete it:

   ```
   val sourceFileName =
   "src${SEPARATOR}main${SEPARATOR}resources${SEPARATOR}file2.txt"
   val sourceFile = File(sourceFileName)

   val targetFileName =
   "src${SEPARATOR}main${SEPARATOR}resources${SEPARATOR}file2_copy.txt
   "
   val targetFile = File(targetFileName)

   if (targetFile.exists()) targetFile.delete()
   ```

5. Copy the contents of `file2.txt` to the `file2_copy.txt` file:

```
val sourceFileName =
"src${SEPARATOR}main${SEPARATOR}resources${SEPARATOR}file2.txt"
val sourceFile = File(sourceFileName)

val targetFileName =
"src${SEPARATOR}main${SEPARATOR}resources${SEPARATOR}file2_copy.txt
"
val targetFile = File(targetFileName)

if (targetFile.exists()) targetFile.delete()

sourceFile.copyTo(targetFile)
```

6. Print both files to the console for verification:

```
val sourceFileName =
"src${SEPARATOR}main${SEPARATOR}resources${SEPARATOR}file2.txt"
val sourceFile = File(sourceFileName)

val targetFileName =
"src${SEPARATOR}main${SEPARATOR}resources${SEPARATOR}file2_copy.txt
"
val targetFile = File(targetFileName)

if (targetFile.exists()) targetFile.delete()

sourceFile.copyTo(targetFile)

File(sourceFileName).readText().apply { println(this) }
File(targetFileName).readText().apply { println(this) }
```

How it works...

You can run the sample code to verify that, after invoking the `copyTo()` extension
function, both files contain the same text content. In our case, we get the following output:

```
"Testing can show the presence of errors, but not their absence." - E. W.
Dijkstra
"Testing can show the presence of errors, but not their absence." - E. W.
Dijkstra
```

Under the hood, the `copyTo()` function reads `InputStream` in the source file to the buffer and writes it to the `OutputStream` target file. Internally, streams are being accessed inside the `use()` function block, which closes them automatically after the operation finishes.

Apart from the target `File` instance, the `copyTo()` function takes two optional parameters—`overwrite: Boolean`, which is set to false by default, and `bufferSize: Int`, which is assigned to the default value. Keep in mind that, whenever some directories on a way to the target file are missing, they will be created. Also, if the target file already exists, the `copyTo()` function will fail, unless the override argument is set to `true`.

- When the `overwrite` parameter is set to `true` and `target` points to a directory, it will be replaced only if it is empty.
- If you invoke `copyTo()` on a `File` instance that points to a directory, it will be copied without its content. Only an empty directory will be created under the target path.
- The `copyTo()` function doesn't preserve copied file attributes, that is, the creation/modification date and permissions.

Traversing files in a directory

In this recipe, we are going to explore how to traverse files in a given directory. We are going to obtain a `FileTreeWalk` class instance from a given `File` pointing to the directory. We are going to iterate through all the files inside the given directory, including any nested subdirectories. We will also filter the files to exclude those without the `.txt` extension and print their paths and contents to the console.

Getting ready

Make sure you have the sample files with the `.txt` extension included in your project. You can clone the sample project provided with the book at the GitHub repository: `https://github.com/PacktPublishing/Kotlin-Standard-Library-Cookbook`. In this recipe, we are going to use the `src/main/resources` directory and its contents from the sample project.

How to do it...

1. Import the `File.separator` constant and assign an alias to it:

   ```
   import java.io.File.separator as SEPARATOR
   ```

2. Obtain the `FileTreeWalk` instance from the `File` pointing to the `src/main/resources` directory:

   ```
   val directoryPath = "src${SEPARATOR}main${SEPARATOR}resources"
   val fileTreeWalk: FileTreeWalk = File(directoryPath).walk()
   ```

3. Iterate through the all non-empty `.txt` files and print:

   ```
   val directoryPath = "src${SEPARATOR}main${SEPARATOR}resources"

   val fileTreeWalk: FileTreeWalk = File(directoryPath).walk()
   fileTreeWalk
           .filter { it.isFile }
           .filter { it.extension == "txt" }
           .filter { it.readBytes().isNotEmpty() }
           .forEach {
               it.apply {
                   println(path)
                   println(readText())
                   println()
               }
           }
   ```

How it works...

We start by instantiating the `File` type instance that references the `src/main/resources` directory and invoking the `walk()` function on it. `walk()` returns the `FileTreeWalk` instance, which is a high-level abstraction layer over the filesystem and allows us to iterate through the files and subdirectories of the original `File` object.

> `FileTreeWalk` extends a `Sequence<File>` interface and provides an `Iterator<File>` implementation, which allows us to iterate through the files and apply any transforming operations to them, in the same way we do while working with collections.

Next, we apply a few filtering operations—removing the `File` objects referencing directories, removing files that don't contain the `.txt` extension, and removing any empty files from the sequence. Finally, we use the `forEach()` function to print the paths of the consecutive files together with their contents.

As you can observe, the default order provided by the `FileTreeWalk` sequence is from top to bottom. We can define a reversed sequence by calling the `walk()` function with a `direction` parameter set to `FileWalkDirection.BOTTOM_UP`.

 There are also two out-of-the-box specialized variants of the `walk()` function available—`File.walkTopDown()` and `File.walkBottomUp()`. The first one returns the `FileTreeWalk` instance with the direction property set to `FileWalkDirection.TOP_DOWN`, and the second one sets `direction` to `FileWalkDirection.BOTTOM_UP`.

7
Making Asynchronous Programming Great Again

In this chapter, we will cover the following recipes:

- Executing tasks in the background using threads
- Background threads synchronization
- Using coroutines for asynchronous, concurrent execution of tasks
- Using coroutines for asynchronous, concurrent tasks execution with results handling
- Applying coroutines for asynchronous data processing
- Easy coroutine cancelation
- Building a REST API client with Retrofit and a coroutines adapter
- Wrapping third-party callback-style APIs with coroutines

Introduction

This chapter is going to address various aspects of asynchronous programming problems. The first two recipes, *Executing tasks in the background using threads* and *Background-threads synchronization*, are going to explain the standard library support for running background tasks using JVM threads.

In the further recipes, we are going to delve more deeply into the powerful Kotlin Coroutines framework. Those recipes are going to explain a general usage of coroutines for asynchronous and concurrent tasks executing. They will also present how to employ coroutines for solving more specific daily-life programming problems, such as concurrent data processing, asynchronous REST-call handling, and working with third-party callback-style APIs in a clean way. After reading this chapter, you will feel convenient applying the coroutines framework to write robust asynchronous code or to optimize your code by running expensive computations concurrently.

The Kotlin Coroutines framework is not only a handy replacement for platform-specific concurrency and async frameworks. Its power is based on providing a unified, universal API that allows us to write asynchronous code, which can be run both on JVM, Android, JavaScript, and native platforms.

Executing tasks in the background using threads

In this recipe, we are going to explore how to work effectively with the JVM `Thread` class in a clean way using the Kotlin standard library functions dedicated to convenient thread-running. We are going to simulate two long-running tasks and execute them concurrently in background threads.

Getting ready

In this recipe, we are going to make use of two functions simulating long-running operations. Here is the first:

```
private fun `5 sec long task`() = Thread.sleep(5000)
```

And here is the second:

```
private fun `2 sec long task`() = Thread.sleep(2000)
```

They are both just responsible for blocking a current thread for five and two seconds, respectively, in order to simulate long-running tasks. We will also make use of the predefined function returning the current thread name for debugging purposes:

```
private fun getCurrentThreadName(): String = Thread.currentThread().name
```

How to do it...

1. Let's start by logging the current thread name to the console:

```
println("Running on ${getCurrentThreadName()}")
```

2. Start a new `Thread` and invoke the `` `5 sec long task` () `` function inside it:

```
println("Running on ${getCurrentThreadName()}")

thread {
    println("Starting async operation on
${getCurrentThreadName()}")
    `5 sec long task`()
    println("Ending async operation on ${getCurrentThreadName()}")
}
```

3. Start another `Thread` and invoke `` `2 sec long task` () `` inside it:

```
println("Running on ${getCurrentThreadName()}")

thread {
    println("Starting async operation on
${getCurrentThreadName()}")
    `5 sec long task`()
    println("Ending async operation on ${getCurrentThreadName()}")
}

thread {
    println("Starting async operation on
${getCurrentThreadName()}")
    `2 sec long task`()
    println("Ending async operation on ${getCurrentThreadName()}")
}
```

How it works...

The preceding code is going to print the following text to the console:

```
Running on main
Starting async operation on Thread-0
Starting async operation on Thread-1
Ending async operation on Thread-1
Ending async operation on Thread-0
```

As you can see, we have successfully started two background threads, which are running concurrently. We are using the `thread()` utility function from the `kotlin.concurrent` package, which is responsible for instantiating and starting a new thread that runs a block of code passed to it in the form of a lambda expression.

See also

- Take a look at the rest of the recipes to discover how to use the Kotlin Coroutines framework to replace the threading mechanism with a more robust and flexible framework. A good starting point could be the *Using coroutines for asynchronous concurrent-tasks execution* and *Using coroutines for asynchronous concurrent-tasks execution with results-handling* recipes.

Background threads synchronization

In this recipe, we are going to explore how to work effectively with the JVM `Thread` class in a clean way using the Kotlin standard library functions dedicated to running threads in a convenient way. We are going to simulate two long-running tasks and execute them in background threads synchronously.

Getting ready

In this recipe, we are going to make use of the following two functions to simulate long-running operations. The `5 sec long task`() function:

```
private fun `5 sec long task`() = Thread.sleep(5000)
```

and the `2 sec long task`() function:

```
private fun `2 sec long task`() = Thread.sleep(2000)
```

They are both just responsible for blocking a current thread for five and two seconds, respectively, in order to simulate long-running tasks. We will also make use of the predefined function returning the current thread name for debugging purposes:

```
private fun getCurrentThreadName(): String = Thread.currentThread().name
```

How to do it...

1. Let's start by logging the current thread name to the console:

   ```
   println("Running on ${getCurrentThreadName()}")
   ```

2. Start a new `Thread` and invoke the `` `5 sec long task` `` () function inside it:

   ```
   println("Running on ${getCurrentThreadName()}")

   thread {
       println("Starting async operation on
   ${getCurrentThreadName()}")
       `5 sec long task`()
       println("Ending async operation on ${getCurrentThreadName()}")
   }
   ```

3. Wait until the thread completes:

   ```
   println("Running on ${getCurrentThreadName()}")

   thread {
       println("Starting async operation on
   ${getCurrentThreadName()}")
       `5 sec long task`()
       println("Ending async operation on ${getCurrentThreadName()}")
   }.join()
   ```

4. Start another `Thread` and invoke `` `2 sec long task` `` () inside it:

   ```
   println("Running on ${getCurrentThreadName()}")

   thread {
       println("Starting async operation on
   ${getCurrentThreadName()}")
       `5 sec long task`()
       println("Ending async operation on ${getCurrentThreadName()}")
   }.join()

   thread {
       println("Starting async operation on
   ${getCurrentThreadName()}")
       `2 sec long task`()
       println("Ending async operation on ${getCurrentThreadName()}")
   }
   ```

5. Wait until the thread completes:

```
println("Running on ${getCurrentThreadName()}")

thread {
    println("Starting async operation on
${getCurrentThreadName()}")
    `5 sec long task`()
    println("Ending async operation on ${getCurrentThreadName()}")
}.join()

thread {
    println("Starting async operation on
${getCurrentThreadName()}")
    `2 sec long task`()
    println("Ending async operation on ${getCurrentThreadName()}")
}.join()
```

6. Test whether the main thread is free at the end:

```
println("Running on ${getCurrentThreadName()}")

thread {
    println("Starting async operation on
${getCurrentThreadName()}")
    `5 sec long task`()
    println("Ending async operation on ${getCurrentThreadName()}")
}.join()

thread {
    println("Starting async operation on
${getCurrentThreadName()}")
    `2 sec long task`()
    println("Ending async operation on ${getCurrentThreadName()}")
}.join()

println("${getCurrentThreadName()} thread is free now")
```

How it works...

The preceding code is going to print the following text to the console:

```
Running on main
Starting async operation on Thread-0
Ending async operation on Thread-0
Starting async operation on Thread-1
```

```
Ending async operation on Thread-1
main thread is free now
```

We have successfully started two background threads, which are synchronized. In order to run both background threads sequentially, we are using the `Thread.join()` function, which just blocks the main thread until the background thread completes. In order to instantiate and start a new background thread, we are using the `thread()` utility function from the `kotlin.concurrent` package. We are passing it a block of code to be run inside the thread inside a lambda expression.

See also

- Take a look at the next recipes explaining how to use the Kotlin Coroutines framework to replace the threading mechanism with a more robust and flexible framework. A good starting point could be the *Using coroutines for asynchronous concurrent-tasks execution* and *Using coroutines for asynchronous concurrent-tasks execution with results-handling* recipes.

Using coroutines for asynchronous, concurrent execution of tasks

In this recipe, we are going to explore how to use the coroutines framework in order to schedule asynchronous, concurrent execution of tasks. We are going to learn both how to synchronize a sequence of short background tasks and how to run expensive, long-running ones at the same time. We will simulate the sushi rolls preparation process to discover how to schedule blocking and non-blocking tasks together.

Getting ready

The first step to start working with Kotlin Coroutines is to add the core framework dependency to the project:

```
implementation 'org.jetbrains.kotlinx:kotlinx-coroutines-core:0.23.3'
```

The preceding code declares the `kotlinx-coroutines-core` dependency in a Gradle build script, which is used in the sample project (`https://github.com/PacktPublishing/Kotlin-Standard-Library-Cookbook`).

In the current recipe, we will assume our sushi-cooking simulation requires the four following steps to be performed:

1. Cook the rice
2. Prepare the fish
3. Cut the vegetables
4. Roll the sushi

These steps are going to be simulated by the following functions:

```
private fun `cook rice`() {
    println("Starting to cook rice on ${getCurrentThreadName()}")
    Thread.sleep(10000)
    println("Rice cooked")
}

private fun `prepare fish`() {
    println("Starting to prepare fish on ${getCurrentThreadName()}")
    Thread.sleep(2000)
    println("Fish prepared")
}

private fun `cut vegetable`() {
    println("Starting to cut vegetables on ${getCurrentThreadName()}")
    Thread.sleep(2000)
    println("Vegetables ready")
}

private fun `roll the sushi`() {
    println("Starting to roll the sushi on ${getCurrentThreadName()}")
    Thread.sleep(2000)
    println("Sushi rolled")
}
```

We will also use the following function to log a current thread name to the console:

```
private fun `print current thread name`() {
    println("Running on ${getCurrentThreadName()}")
    println()
}

private fun getCurrentThreadName(): String = Thread.currentThread().name
```

For the sake of the exercise, we will assume the sushi-roll preparation process must fulfill the following requirements:

- The longest *Rice-cooking* step must be executed in the background in a non-blocking way
- The *Fish-preparation* and *Vegetable-cutting* steps have to be performed one by one while the rice is cooking
- The *Sushi-rolling* step can be done only when the first three steps are completed

How to do it...

1. Let's start by logging the current thread name to the console:

```
`print current thread name`()
```

2. Start a new coroutine running on a pool of background threads:

```
`print current thread name`()
var sushiCookingJob: Job
sushiCookingJob = launch(newSingleThreadContext("SushiThread")) {
    `print current thread name`()
}
```

3. Execute the `cook rice`() function asynchronously in a nested coroutine:

```
`print current thread name`()
var sushiCookingJob: Job
sushiCookingJob = launch(newSingleThreadContext("SushiThread")) {
    `print current thread name`()
    val riceCookingJob = launch {
        `cook rice`()
    }
}
```

4. Run the `prepare fish`() and `cut vegetable`() functions sequentially while the `cook rice`() function is running in the background:

```
`print current thread name`()
var sushiCookingJob: Job
sushiCookingJob = launch(newSingleThreadContext("SushiThread")) {
    `print current thread name`()
    val riceCookingJob = launch {
        `cook rice`()
    }
    println("Current thread is not blocked while rice is being
```

```
    cooked")
    `prepare fish` ()
    `cut vegetable` ()
}
```

5. Wait until the rice-cooking coroutine completes:

```
`print current thread name` ()
var sushiCookingJob: Job
sushiCookingJob = launch(newSingleThreadContext("SushiThread")) {
    `print current thread name` ()
    val riceCookingJob = launch {
        `cook rice` ()
    }
    println("Current thread is not blocked while rice is being
     cooked")
    `prepare fish` ()
    `cut vegetable` ()
    riceCookingJob.join()
}
```

6. Invoke the final `roll the sushi` () function and wait until the main coroutine completes:

```
`print current thread name` ()
var sushiCookingJob: Job
sushiCookingJob = launch(newSingleThreadContext("SushiThread")) {
    `print current thread name` ()
    val riceCookingJob = launch {
        `cook rice` ()
    }
    println("Current thread is not blocked while rice is being
     cooked")
    `prepare fish` ()
    `cut vegetable` ()
    riceCookingJob.join()
    `roll the sushi` ()
}
runBlocking {
    sushiCookingJob.join()
}
```

7. Measure the total time for function execution and log it to the console:

```
`print current thread name` ()
var sushiCookingJob: Job
val time = measureTimeMillis {
    sushiCookingJob = launch(newSingleThreadContext("SushiThread"))
```

```
    {
        `print current thread name`()
        val riceCookingJob = launch {
            `cook rice`()
        }
        println("Current thread is not blocked while rice is being
         cooked")
        `prepare fish`()
        `cut vegetable`()
        riceCookingJob.join()
        `roll the sushi`()
    }
    runBlocking {
        sushiCookingJob.join()
    }
}
println("Total time: $time ms")
```

How it works...

The preceding code is going to print the following text to the console:

```
Running on main
Running on SushiThread
Current thread is not blocked while rice is being cooked
Starting to cook rice on ForkJoinPool.commonPool-worker-1
Starting to prepare fish on SushiThread
Fish prepared
Starting to cut vegetables on SushiThread
Vegetables ready
Rice cooked
Starting to roll the sushi on SushiThread
Sushi rolled
Total time: 12089 ms
```

In the beginning, we start a new coroutine running on a background thread with the launch() function call. We also create a handle to the Job instance returned by the launch() function under the var sushiCookingJob: Job variable.

The `launch()` function starts a new coroutine instance on a default `CoroutineContext` instance. However, we are able to pass our desired `CoroutineContext` as an additional parameter to the `launch()` function. When targeting the JVM platform, by default the `launch()` function starts a coroutine on a pool of background threads, which corresponds to the `CommonPool` context constant. We can also run the coroutine on a single thread by passing a context result of the `newSingleThreadContext()` function. If you are working with UI frameworks, such as Android, Swing, or JavaFx, you can run a coroutine on a `UI` context as well. The `UI` context is related to the main thread responsible for user-interface updates. There are different modules that provide the `UI` context implementation dedicated to a specific framework. You can learn more about framework-specific UI programming with coroutines in the following official guide: `https://github.com/Kotlin/kotlinx.coroutines/blob/master/ui/coroutines-guide-ui.md`.

Inside the main coroutine, we are starting a new one and invoking the `cook rice`() function inside it. We are storing a handle to the `Job` instance corresponding to the coroutine handling the `cook rice`() function under the `val riceCookingJob: Job` variable. At this point, the rice-cooking task begins to run concurrently on a pool of threads.

Next, we are invoking two functions—`prepare fish`() and `cut vegetable`(). As you can see in the console output, those functions are executed sequentially. The vegetable-cutting task starts right after the fish-preparation completes. If we'd like to run them concurrently, we'd need to start each one inside a new coroutine.

Finally, we wait for the completion of the rice-cooking task by calling a `join()` function on the `riceCookingJob` variable. Here, the `join()` function suspends the primary `sushiCookingJob` coroutine until `riceCookingJob` is complete. Right after the primary coroutine gets unblocked, the last `roll the sushi`() function is invoked.

In order to await the primary coroutine completion, we need to invoke a `join()` function on the `sushiCookingJob` instance after starting it on the main thread. However, we are not able to call the `join()` function outside of a coroutine scope. We need to call it inside a new *blocking* coroutine started with a `runBlocking()` function.

The coroutines framework is designed to allow us to execute tasks in a non-blocking way. Although we are able to write non-blocking code inside a coroutine's scope, we need to provide a bridge to the original thread inside the application that starts the primary coroutine. We are able to connect the non-blocking coroutine scope with the blocking world outside using the runBlocking() function.

The runBlocking() function starts a new coroutine and blocks the current thread until its completion. It is designed to bridge regular blocking code to libraries that are written in suspending style. For example, it can be used in main() functions and in tests.

Coroutines can be seen as lightweight thread replacements. Coroutines are lightweight in terms of resource consumption. For example, we can start a million coroutines concurrently with ease, where, after a second, each of them logs the current thread name to the console:

```
runBlocking {
    (0..1000000).map {
        launch {
            delay(1000)
            println("Running on ${Thread.currentThread().name}")
        }
    }.map { it.join() }
}
```

The preceding code will complete in about 10 seconds on a standard computer. In contrast, if we try to run this code using threads, we get the OutOfMemoryError: unable to create new native thread exception.

See also

- You can follow up by reading the *Using coroutines for asynchronous, concurrent tasks execution with results handling* recipe. It shows you how to asynchronously schedule functions that return the results.

Using coroutines for asynchronous, concurrent tasks execution with results handling

In this recipe, we are going to explore how to use the coroutines framework in order to run asynchronous operations concurrently, and learn how to handle the results they return properly. We are going to schedule two tasks and run them in the background using two coroutines. The first task is going to be responsible for displaying the progress-bar animation. The second one is going to simulate long-running computations. In the end, we are going to print the results returned by the second task to the console.

Getting ready

The first step to start working with Kotlin Coroutines is to add a core framework dependency to the project:

```
implementation 'org.jetbrains.kotlinx:kotlinx-coroutines-core:0.23.3'
```

The preceding code declares the `kotlinx-coroutines-core` dependency in a Gradle build script, which is used in the sample project (https://github.com/PacktPublishing/Kotlin-Standard-Library-Cookbook).

In the current recipe, we are going to make use of the following two functions:

```
private suspend fun `calculate the answer to life the universe and
everything`(): Int {
    delay(5000)
    return 42
}

private suspend fun `show progress animation`() {
    val progressBarLength = 30
    var currentPosition = 0
    while (true) {
        print("\r")
        val progressbar = (0 until progressBarLength)
                .map { if (it == currentPosition) " " else "▓" }
                .joinToString("")
        print(progressbar)

        delay(50)
```

```
        if (currentPosition == progressBarLength) {
            currentPosition = 0
        }
        currentPosition++
    }
}
```

The first one is simulating an expensive computation that delays a thread for five seconds and returns the result in the end. The second one is responsible for displaying an infinite progress-bar animation. We are going to start both operations concurrently and wait for the result returned by the first one. After we get the result, we will print it to the console.

We will also use the following function to log a current thread name to the console:

```
private fun `print current thread name`() {
    println("Running on ${getCurrentThreadName()}")
    println()
}

private fun getCurrentThreadName(): String = Thread.currentThread().name
```

How to do it...

1. Start by logging a current thread name to the console:

   ```
   `print current thread name`()
   ```

2. Start a coroutine responsible for displaying progress-bar animation from the background:

   ```
   `print current thread name`()

   launch {
       println("Starting progressbar animation on
   ${getCurrentThreadName()}")
       `show progress animation`()
   }
   ```

3. Start a coroutine responsible for running the `calculate the answer to life the universe and everything`() function in the background:

   ```
   `print current thread name`()

   launch {
       println("Starting progressbar animation on
   ```

```
${getCurrentThreadName()}")
    `show progress animation`()
}

val future = async {
    println("Starting computations on ${getCurrentThreadName()}")
    `calculate the answer to life the universe and everything`()
}

println("${getCurrentThreadName()} thread is not blocked while
tasks are in progress")
```

4. Wait for the result returned by the `future` coroutine and print it to the console:

```
`print current thread name`()

launch {
    println("Starting progressbar animation on
${getCurrentThreadName()}")
    `show progress animation`()
}

val future = async {
    println("Starting computations on ${getCurrentThreadName()}")
    `calculate the answer to life the universe and everything`()
}

println("${getCurrentThreadName()} thread is not blocked while
tasks are in progress")

runBlocking {
    println("\nThe answer to life the universe and everything:
${future.await()}")
    `print current thread name`()
}
```

How it works...

Our code is going to display the progress-bar animation for five seconds and then print the result of the `calculate the answer to life the universe and everything`() function once it completes the simulated calculations:

```
Running on main
Starting progressbar animation on ForkJoinPool.commonPool-worker-1
Starting calculation of the answer to life the universe and everything on
ForkJoinPool.commonPool-worker-2
```

```
main thread is not blocked while background tasks are still in progress

The answer to life the universe and everything: 42
Running on main
```

We start the execution of `calculate the answer to life the universe and everything` () in the background task using the async() function. It just starts a new coroutine and returns an instance of a Deferred<T> class. The generic T type corresponds to the type of object that is returned by async(). An instance of the Deferred<T> type is just a pointer to the future result delivered by the coroutine. It's a representation of asynchronous programming constructs, called *futures* or *promises*. We are able to evaluate the value of a Deferred object by calling the await() function on it. However, we are not able to call the await() function outside a coroutine scope. We need to call it inside a new *blocking* coroutine started with a runBlocking() function.

The coroutines framework is designed to allow us to execute tasks in a non-blocking way. Although we are able to write non-blocking code inside a coroutine's scope, we need to provide a bridge to the original thread inside the application that starts the primary coroutine. We are able to connect the non-blocking coroutine scope with the blocking world outside using the runBlocking() function.

The runBlocking() function starts a new coroutine and blocks the current thread until its completion. It is designed to bridge regular blocking code to libraries that are written in suspending style. For example, it can be used in main() functions and in tests.

As far as the progress-bar animation is concerned, we are scheduling it in the background using the launch() function. launch() is responsible for starting a new coroutine, however, it does not care about delivering the final results.

There's more...

You may have noticed our predefined functions are marked with the suspend modifier declared before the fun keyword, for example, **suspend** fun `show progress animation` (). The reason behind this is that we need to declare explicitly that the function is going to run inside the coroutine scope to be able to use coroutine-specific features inside the function's body. In our case, we are using the delay() function, which can be invoked only inside a coroutine scope. It is responsible for pausing the coroutine for a given amount of time without blocking the current thread.

See also

- You can investigate another usage of the `delay()` function in the *Applying coroutines for asynchronous data processing* recipe. You can also explore different use cases of suspending functions in the *Easy coroutines cancelation* recipe.
- If you'd like to learn more about concurrent, asynchronous tasks-scheduling with coroutines, you can take a look at the *Using coroutines for asynchronous, concurrent tasks execution with results handling* recipe. It explains how to schedule both sequential and concurrent tasks running in a common coroutine.

Applying coroutines for asynchronous data processing

In this recipe, we are going to implement a generic extension for the `Iterable` type, which will provide a replacement for the `Iterable<T>.map()` function. Our implementation of the `Iterable<T>.mapConcurrent()` function is going to allow data-mapping-operation optimization by running it concurrently with coroutines. Next, we are going to test our concurrent mapping function implementation by employing it to perform a simulation of a time-expensive operation applied to each of the elements of a sample `Iterable` object.

How to do it...

1. Implement an extension function for the generic `Iterable<T>` class responsible for handling the mapping operation of its elements concurrently:

```
suspend fun <T, R> Iterable<T>.mapConcurrent(transform: suspend (T)
-> R) =
    this.map {
        async { transform(it) }
    }.map {
        it.await()
    }
```

2. Simulate time-consuming mapping operations applied to the sample `Iterable` range elements:

```
runBlocking {
    (0..10).mapConcurrent {
```

```
            delay(1000)
            it * it
        }
    }
```

3. Print the mapped elements to the console:

```
runBlocking {
        (0..10).mapConcurrent {
            delay(1000)
            it * it
        }.map { println(it) }
    }
```

4. Measure the total time of the concurrent-mapping operation's execution and log it to the console:

```
runBlocking {
    val totalTime = measureTimeMillis {
        (0..10).mapConcurrent {
            delay(1000)
            it * it
        }.map { println(it) }
    }
    println("Total time: $totalTime ms")
}
```

How it works...

Let's start by analyzing the effects of applying the mapConcurrent() function we implemented at the beginning to transform elements of the (0..10) range of integers. In the lambda block passed to themapConcurrent function, we are simulating a long-running processing operation suspending the coroutine for one second, using the delay(1000) function and returning a square of the original integer value.

Our code is going to print the following results to the console:

```
0
1
4
9
16
25
36
49
64
```

```
81
100
Total time: 1040 ms
```

Our implementation of the `Iterable.mapConcurrent()` extension function takes a functional parameter, `transform: suspend (T) -> R`, which represents an operation that is going to be applied to each element of the original of the `Iterable` object. Under the hood, in order to perform data transformation concurrently, there is a new coroutine started for each of the original elements using the `async()` function, and the `transform` function is applied to them. At this point, the original `Iterable<T>` instance has been transformed to the `Iterable<Deferred<T>>` type. Next, the instances of the consecutive `Deferred` type, returned by invocations of `async()`, are synchronized and transformed to the generic `R` type by calling the `await()` functions on them. In the end, we have an `Iterable` of the desired `R` type returned.

As you can see, in the output of our example, the transformation of 10 integer numbers using the `Iterable.mapConcurrent()` function took roughly one second on a standard computer. You can try running the same transformations using the standard `Iterable.map()` and it will take around 10 seconds.

In order to simulate the delay inside the `transform` lambda block passed to the `mapConcurrent()` function, we use the `delay()` function with a specified time value passed. The `delay()` is suspending the coroutine for a given amount of time, but it's not blocking a thread. The `transform` block is being executed for each of the elements on the pool of background threads. Whenever one coroutine is suspended, another one is starting to run in place of the first one. If we replace the non-blocking `delay(1000)` call with the blocking `Thread.sleep(1000)` function, our example will finish in about four seconds. It is still a big win compared to the standard `Iterable.map()` function which doesn't run concurrently by default.

The coroutines framework is designed to allow us to execute tasks in a non-blocking way. Although we are able to write non-blocking code inside a coroutine's scope, we need to provide a bridge to the original thread inside the application that starts the primary coroutine. We are able to connect the non-blocking coroutine scope with the blocking world outside using the `runBlocking()` function.

The `runBlocking()` function starts a new coroutine and blocks the current thread until its completion. It is designed to bridge regular blocking code to libraries that are written in suspending style. For example, it can be used in `main()` functions and in tests.

See also

- If you'd like to learn more about the basics of the extension function mechanism, you can take a look at the *Extending functionalities of classes* recipe in `Chapter 2`, *Expressive Functions and Adjustable Interfaces*

Easy coroutine cancelation

In this recipe, we are going to explore how to implement a coroutine that allows us to cancel its execution. We are going to create an infinite progress-bar animation running in the console in the background using a coroutine. Next, after a given delay, we are going to cancel the coroutine and test how the animation behaves.

Getting ready

The first step to start working with Kotlin Coroutines is to add a core framework dependency to the project:

```
implementation 'org.jetbrains.kotlinx:kotlinx-coroutines-core:0.23.3'
```

The preceding code declares the `kotlinx-coroutines-core` dependency in a Gradle build script, which is used in the sample project (`https://github.com/PacktPublishing/Kotlin-Standard-Library-Cookbook`).

How to do it...

1. Implement a suspend function responsible for displaying an infinite progress-bar animation in the console:

```
private suspend fun `show progress animation`() {
    val progressBarLength = 30
    var currentPosition = 0
    while (true) {
        print("\r")
        val progressbar = (0 until progressBarLength)
                .map { if (it == currentPosition) " " else "▓" }
                .joinToString("")
        print(progressbar)

        delay(50)
```

```
            if (currentPosition == progressBarLength) {
                currentPosition = 0
            }
            currentPosition++
        }
    }
```

2. Launch the `show progress animation`() function inside a new coroutine:

```
runBlocking {
    val job = launch { `show progress animation`() }
}
```

3. Delay the parent thread by five seconds:

```
runBlocking {
    val job = launch { `show progress animation`() }
    delay(5000)
}
```

4. Cancel the progress-bar animation job:

```
runBlocking {
    val job = launch { `show progress animation`() }
    delay(5000)
    job.cancel()
    println("Cancelled")
}
```

5. Wait for the job to complete and log the completion event to the console:

```
runBlocking {
    val job = launch {`show progress animation`()}
    delay(5000)
    job.cancel()
    job.join()
    println("\nJob cancelled and completed")
}
```

How it works...

In the end, our code is going to display a progress-bar animation for five seconds and then stop it. We are scheduling the `show progress animation`() function to run in the background by invoking it inside a new coroutine instance created by the launch() function. We are storing a handle to a Job instance returned by the launch() function under the job variable.

Next, we are suspending the outer `runBlocking()` coroutine scope by five seconds with the `delay(5000)` call. Once the `delay()` function resumes coroutine execution, we call the `cancel()` function on the coroutine `Job` responsible for displaying the progress-bar animation.

Under the hood, inside the `` `show progress animation` `` () function, we are running an infinite `while` loop, which updates the last console line with a new progress-bar animation state every 50 milliseconds. However, as you can verify by running the example, the animation stops immediately after the corresponding `Job` responsible for running it gets canceled, even though, after the cancellation, we invoke the `join()` function to wait for its completion.

> You can also make use of a `Job` extension function, called `cancelAndJoin()`, that combines the `cancel()` and `join()` calls together. However, if you don't want to wait for the actual coroutine stop-event, a simple `cancel()` call is enough.

See also

- If you'd like to explore the basics of the coroutines framework, take a look at the *Using coroutines for asynchronous concurrent-tasks execution* and *Using coroutines for asynchronous concurrent-tasks execution with results-handling* recipes

Building a REST API client with Retrofit and a coroutines adapter

In this recipe, we are going to explore how to employ coroutines to interact with remote endpoints using REST APIs. We are going to implement a REST client using the Retrofit library, allowing us to communicate over HTTP with the GitHub API asynchronously. Finally, we will use it in practice to fetch GitHub repositories search results for a given search query.

Getting ready

The first step to start working with Kotlin Coroutines is to add a core framework dependency:

```
implementation 'org.jetbrains.kotlinx:kotlinx-coroutines-core:0.23.3'
```

In order to make use of the Retrofit library with the coroutines adapter plugin, we also need to add the following dependencies to our project:

```
implementation 'com.squareup.retrofit2:retrofit:2.4.0'
implementation 'com.squareup.retrofit2:converter-gson:2.4.0'
implementation 'com.jakewharton.retrofit:retrofit2-kotlin-coroutines-
experimental-adapter:1.0.0'
```

The preceding code declares the required dependencies in a Gradle build script, which is used in a sample project (https://github.com/PacktPublishing/Kotlin-Standard-Library-Cookbook). The retrofit module provides the core Retrofit library implementation. converter-gson adds a Gson plugin that enables automatic conversion of the JSON response to Kotlin model-data classes. The retrofit2-kotlin-coroutines-experimental-adapter module provides an adapter for async REST calls, allowing us to wrap the response using the Kotlin Coroutines Deferred type.

In this recipe, we are going to use the GitHub REST API, which is available publicly. We are going to communicate with an endpoint responsible for returning search results containing GitHub repositories for a given search query. You can find detailed endpoint docs here: https://developer.github.com/v3/search/#search-repositories.

The /search/repositories endpoint allows us to access the remote resources using the GET method and passing the desired search phrase under the key, called q. For example, the URL with the GET request for repositories matching the "live.parrot" search phrase would look like this:
https://api.github.com/search/repositories?q=parrot.live. The results delivered by the endpoint are formatted using the JSON format. You can check out how the raw response looks like by opening the example URL in your browser or using the curl command-line tool: curl
https://api.github.com/search/repositories?q=parrot.live.

How to do it...

1. Declare data classes modeling the server response:

```
data class Response(@SerializedName("items")
                                    val list:
Collection<Repository>)
data class Repository(val id: Long?,
                      val name: String?,
                      val description: String?,
                      @SerializedName("full_name") val fullName:
                       String?,
                      @SerializedName("html_url") val url: String?,
                      @SerializedName("stargazers_count") val
stars:
                      Long?)
```

2. Declare an interface modeling the GitHub endpoint usage:

```
interface GithubApi {
    @GET("/search/repositories")
    fun searchRepositories(@Query("q") searchQuery: String):
    Deferred<Response>

}
```

3. Instantiate the `GithubApi` interface using the `Retrofit` class:

```
val api: GithubApi = Retrofit.Builder()
        .baseUrl("https://api.github.com/")
        .addConverterFactory(GsonConverterFactory.create())
        .addCallAdapterFactory(CoroutineCallAdapterFactory())
        .build()
        .create(GithubApi::class.java)
```

4. Make a call to the endpoint using the `GithubApi` instance and pass `"kotlin"` as a search phrase:

```
val api: GithubApi = Retrofit.Builder()
        .baseUrl("https://api.github.com/")
        .addConverterFactory(GsonConverterFactory.create())
        .addCallAdapterFactory(CoroutineCallAdapterFactory())
        .build()
        .create(GithubApi::class.java)

api.searchRepositories("Kotlin")
```

5. Wait for the response and get a reference to the obtained list of `Repository` class objects:

```
val api: GithubApi = Retrofit.Builder()
        .baseUrl("https://api.github.com/")
        .addConverterFactory(GsonConverterFactory.create())
        .addCallAdapterFactory(CoroutineCallAdapterFactory())
        .build()
        .create(GithubApi::class.java)

val downloadedRepos = api.searchRepositories("Kotlin").await().list
```

6. Sort the repositories list by the number of their stars count in decreasing order, and print them to the console:

```
val api: GithubApi = Retrofit.Builder()
        .baseUrl("https://api.github.com/")
        .addConverterFactory(GsonConverterFactory.create())
        .addCallAdapterFactory(CoroutineCallAdapterFactory())
        .build()
        .create(GithubApi::class.java)

val downloadedRepos = api.searchRepositories("Kotlin").await().list
downloadedRepos
  .sortedByDescending { it.stars }
  .forEach {
  it.apply {
  println("$fullName ⭐ $stars\n$description\n$url\n")
  }
  }
```

How it works...

As a result, our code is going to send a request to the server, fetch and process the response, and print the following results to the console:

```
JetBrains/kotlin ⭐ 23051
The Kotlin Programming Language
https://github.com/JetBrains/kotlin

perwendel/spark ⭐ 7531
A simple expressive web framework for java. News: Spark now has a kotlin
DSL https://github.com/perwendel/spark-kotlin
https://github.com/perwendel/spark
```

```
KotlinBy/awesome-kotlin ★5098
A curated list of awesome Kotlin related stuff Inspired by awesome-java.
https://github.com/KotlinBy/awesome-kotlin

ReactiveX/RxKotlin ★4413
RxJava bindings for Kotlin
https://github.com/ReactiveX/RxKotlin

JetBrains/kotlin-native ★4334
Kotlin/Native infrastructure
https://github.com/JetBrains/kotlin-native

. . .
```

We have started by implementing model classes that represent the data returned in the server's JSON response. You may have seen that some of the properties are marked with the `@SerializedName()` annotation. The aim of this annotation is to indicate to the Gson library that the specified property should be deserialized from a JSON field which name matches the value passed to `@SerializedName()`. Next, we are declaring an interface, `GithubApi`, that represents the methods we want to use to communicate with the endpoint. We've declared a single method, called `searchRepositories`, which takes a `String` parameter that corresponds to the search-query value required by the repositories search endpoint. We've also marked the `searchRepositories` method with the `@GET` annotation, which specifies the REST method type to use and a path to the endpoint. The `searchRepositories` method should return an instance of a `Deferred<Response>` type, representing a *future* result of an asynchronous call. Implementation of the `GithubApi` interface is generated by the Retrofit library internally. In order to obtain the `GithubApi` instance, we need to instantiate the `Retrofit` type and configure it with the endpoint's URL address and mechanisms responsible for JSON deserializing and performing asynchronous calls to the server. Finally, we call `Retrofit.create(GithubApi::class.java)` to obtain the `GithubApi` instance. That's it!

In order to execute the actual call to the server, we need to call the `GithubApi.searchRepositories()` function:

```
api.searchRepositories("Kotlin")
```

Next, in order to obtain a list of `Repository` objects from the response, we need to wait for the completion of the async call to the server and response parsing:

```
val downloadedRepos = api.searchRepositories("Kotlin").await().list
```

Finally, we post-process the list of repositories obtained from the response. We are sorting it by the stars count, in decreasing order, and printing it to the console with the following code:

```
val downloadedRepos = api.searchRepositories("Kotlin").await().list
downloadedRepos
        .sortedByDescending { it.stars }
        .forEach {
            it.apply {
                println("$fullName ★ $stars\n$description\n$url\n")
            }
        }
```

See also

- If you'd like to explore the basics of the coroutines framework, take a look at the *Using coroutines for asynchronous concurrent-tasks execution* and *Using coroutines for asynchronous, concurrent tasks execution with results handling* recipes. You can learn more about the Retrofit library by exploring its homepage, `http://square.github.io/retrofit/`, which contains useful examples.

Wrapping third-party callback-style APIs with coroutines

Often third-party libraries offer callback-style asynchronous APIs. However, the callback functions are considered to be an anti-pattern, especially whenever we are dealing with a number of nested callbacks. In this recipe, we are going to learn how to deal with libraries that provide callback-style methods by transforming them easily into suspending functions that can be run using coroutines.

Getting ready

The first step to start working with Kotlin Coroutines is to add the core framework dependency to the project:

```
implementation 'org.jetbrains.kotlinx:kotlinx-coroutines-core:0.23.3'
```

The preceding code declares the `kotlinx-coroutines-core` dependency in a Gradle build script, which is used in the sample project (`https://github.com/PacktPublishing/Kotlin-Standard-Library-Cookbook`).

As far as the recipe task is concerned, let's assume we have a class called `Result`, defined as follows:

```
data class Result(val displayName: String)
```

Here is the `getResultsAsync()` function, which simulates the third-party callback-style API:

```
fun getResultsAsync(callback: (List<Result>) -> Unit) =
    thread {
        val results = mutableListOf<Result>()

        // Simulate some extensive bacground task
        Thread.sleep(1000)

        results.add(Result("a"))
        results.add(Result("b"))
        results.add(Result("c"))

        callback(results)
    }
```

The `getResultsAsync()` function just starts a background thread, delays it for a second, and invokes a callback function passed to it as an argument delivering the list of the `Result` class object to it.

How to do it...

1. Wrap the `getResultsAsync()` function with the suspend function, returning the results directly:

```
suspend fun getResults(): List<Result> =
    suspendCoroutine { continuation: Continuation<List<Result>> ->
```

```
                        getResultsAsync { continuation.resume(it) }
            }
```

2. Start a coroutine and invoke the `getResults()` suspending function inside it:

```
        val asyncResults = async {
            getResults()
        }
```

3. Wait for the results and print them to the console:

```
        val asyncResults = async {
            getResults()
        }

        println("getResults() is running in bacground. Main thread is not
        blocked.")
        asyncResults.await().map { println(it.displayName) }
        println("getResults() completed")
```

How it works...

In the end, our code is going to print the following output to the console:

```
getResults() is running in bacground. Main thread is not blocked.
a
b
c
getResults() completed
Total time elapsed: 1029 ms
```

We've successfully managed to transform the callback-style
`getResultsAsync(callback: (List<Result>) -> Unit)` function into the clean form
of a suspending function returning the results directly–`suspend fun getResults():`
`List<Result>`. In order to get rid of the original `callback` argument, we have used the
`suspendCoroutine()` function provided by the standard library. The
`suspendCoroutine()` function takes the `block: (Continuation<T>) -> Unit`
function type as an argument. The `Continuation` interface is designed to allow us to
resume the coroutine paused by a suspending function.

When the `suspendCoroutine` function is called inside a coroutine, it captures its execution state in a `Continuation` instance and passes this continuation to the specified block as an argument. To resume execution of the coroutine, the block may invoke either `continuation.resume()` or `continuation.resumeWithException()`.

We invoke the original `getResultsAcync()` function inside the lambda passed to the `suspendCoroutine()` function, and we call the `continuation.resume(it)` function in the `callback` lambda blocked passed to the `getResultsAsync()` function as an argument:

```
suspend fun getResults(): List<Result> =
    suspendCoroutine { continuation: Continuation<List<Result>> ->
        getResultsAsync { continuation.resume(it) }
    }
```

As the result, the coroutine inside which `getResults()` is called will become suspended until the `callback` lambda is executed internally in the `getResultsAsync()` function.

See also

- If you'd like to explore the basics of the coroutines framework, take a look at the *Using coroutines for asynchronous, concurrent tasks execution* and *Using coroutines for asynchronous, concurrent tasks execution with results handling* recipes

Best Practices for the Android, JUnit, and JVM UI Frameworks

8

In this chapter, we will cover the following recipes:

- Clean and safe `View` binding with the Android Extensions plugin
- Applying coroutines for asynchronous UI programming on Android, JavaFX, and Swing
- Easy class-serialization on Android using the `@Parcelize` annotation
- Implementing a custom property delegate that provides lifecycle-aware values
- Easy operations on `SharedPreferences`
- Less boilerplate `Cursor` data parsing
- Mocking dependencies with the Mockito Kotlin library
- Verifying function invocations
- Unit tests for Kotlin coroutines

Introduction

The current chapter is going to address problems specific to the popular frameworks that Kotlin uses most often. In general, it is going to focus on Android platform-specific aspects and asynchronous UI programming with coroutines both on the Android and JVM frameworks, such as JavaFX and Swing. It will also guide you through writing effective unit tests for the JVM platform using the JUnit framework (`https://junit.org/junit5/`). The recipes related to unit-testing will include also more advanced topics, such as mocking dependencies with the `mockito-kotlin` (`https://github.com/nhaarman/mockito-kotlin`) library, testing asynchronous code based on the coroutines framework, and working with assertions provided by the standard library.

Clean and safe view-binding with the Android Extensions plugin

In this recipe, we are going to explore the view-binding feature provided by the Kotlin Android Extensions plugin. It allows us to obtain references to `View` type elements declared in the XML layout files in an easy and robust way, without using the original `findViewById()` function. We are going to declare a `TextView` element in the `Activity` layout and obtain a reference to it in order to display a sample text in it.

Getting ready

In order to make use of the Kotlin Android Extensions plugin, we need to enable it in the Android project module-level `build.gradle` script by adding the following declaration:

```
apply plugin: 'kotlin-android-extensions'
```

You can examine the implementation and configuration of recipes related to the Android framework in the AndroidSamples project available in this book's GitHub repository: `https://github.com/PacktPublishing/Kotlin-Standard-Library-Cookbook/`. To follow the Android-related recipes, you just need to create a new project in Android Studio.

How to do it...

1. Create a new Activity in the project:

```
class MainActivity : AppCompatActivity() {}
```

2. Implement the UI layout in the `activity_main.xml` file under the `src/main/res/layout/` directory:

```
<?xml version="1.0" encoding="utf-8"?>
<androidx.constraintlayout.widget.ConstraintLayout
xmlns:android="http://schemas.android.com/apk/res/android"
    xmlns:app="http://schemas.android.com/apk/res-auto"
    xmlns:tools="http://schemas.android.com/tools"
    android:layout_width="match_parent"
    android:layout_height="match_parent"
    tools:context=".MainActivity">

<TextView
```

```
        android:id="@+id/text_field"
        android:layout_width="wrap_content"
        android:layout_height="wrap_content"
        android:textSize="56sp"
        app:layout_constraintBottom_toBottomOf="parent"
        app:layout_constraintLeft_toLeftOf="parent"
        app:layout_constraintRight_toRightOf="parent"
        app:layout_constraintTop_toTopOf="parent" />

</androidx.constraintlayout.widget.ConstraintLayout>
```

3. Set the layout for the `MainActivity` inside the `onCreate()` hook function:

```
class MainActivity : AppCompatActivity() {
    override fun onCreate(savedInstanceState: Bundle?) {
        super.onCreate(savedInstanceState)
        setContentView(R.layout.activity_main)
    }
}
```

4. Get a reference to the `TextView` declared in the XML layout and display a sample text in it:

```
class MainActivity : AppCompatActivity() {
    override fun onCreate(savedInstanceState: Bundle?) {
        super.onCreate(savedInstanceState)
        setContentView(R.layout.activity_main)
        text_field.text = "Bonjour!"
    }
}
```

How it works...

As the result, the `MainActivity` class is going to display a greeting inside `TextView`:

Under the hood, the Android Extensions plugin has generated extension properties for the `MainActivity` class for each of the `View` elements declared in the `activity_main.xml` file. The generated properties have the same names as the IDs of their corresponding layout elements.

Compared to the standard way of obtaining references to `View` classes using the `findViewById(): View` function, the Android Extensions binding mechanism is much cleaner and more painless. It is also safe and robust as it does not require casting the `View` type to specific subclasses, and it regenerates all the extension properties whenever any changes are made to the XML layout files. Also, compared to other third-party view-binding libraries, it is much easier to use as it doesn't require any manual property declarations. It just works seamlessly.

There's more...

By default, the Android Extensions plugin supports the `Activity`, `Fragment`, and `View` type containers where you can use the automatic view binding mechanism out of the box. However, there is a possibility to use any class as an Android Extensions container, by implementing the `LayoutContainer` interface. For example, it can be used in the `RecyclerView.ViewHolder` subclasses:

```
class ViewHolder(override val containerView: View) :
ViewHolder(containerView),
    LayoutContainer {
    fun setupItemView(title: String) {  itemTitle.text = "Hello World!"  }
}
```

 You can learn more about Android Extensions applications in the official reference: https://kotlinlang.org/docs/tutorials/android-plugin. html.

Applying coroutines for asynchronous UI programming on Android, JavaFX, and Swing

Most of the JVM-based GUI frameworks have one thing in common—they run a specific thread that is responsible for updating the state of the application's UI. In this recipe, we're going to learn how to execute tasks asynchronously in the background and switch to the UI thread to update the GUI of the app. We're going to create a simple counter, which is going to display the incremented integer value every second. The mechanism responsible for infinite counter-incrementing should operate in the background, however, it should switch to the UI thread context every time it needs to perform an update of the UI state.

Getting ready

The first step to start working with Kotlin Coroutines is to add the core-framework dependency to the project:

```
implementation 'org.jetbrains.kotlinx:kotlinx-coroutines-core:0.23.3'
```

Apart from the Coroutines core dependency, we will need to add one of the framework-specific coroutines sub-modules, providing the coroutine-context implementation responsible for dispatching the coroutine on the UI thread. You can find the list of coroutines' framework sub-modules in the official guide: `https://github.com/Kotlin/kotlinx.coroutines/blob/master/ui/coroutines-guide-ui.md`. In this recipe, we are going to target the Android platform, however, you can easily port the sample code to one of the supported frameworks such as, Android, Swing, or JavaFx.

You can examine the implementation and configuration of recipes related to the Android framework in the AndroidSamples project, available in the GitHub repository: `https://github.com/PacktPublishing/Kotlin-Standard-Library-Cookbook/`. To follow Android-related recipes, you just need to create a new project in Android Studio.

How to do it...

1. Add a new Activity subclass:

   ```
   class MainActivity: AppCompatActivity() {}
   ```

2. Implement the UI layout in the `activity_main.xml` file under the `src/main/res/layout/` directory:

   ```xml
   <?xml version="1.0" encoding="utf-8"?>
   <androidx.constraintlayout.widget.ConstraintLayout
   xmlns:android="http://schemas.android.com/apk/res/android"
       xmlns:app="http://schemas.android.com/apk/res-auto"
       android:layout_width="match_parent"
       android:layout_height="match_parent" >

   <TextView
       android:id="@+id/text_field"
       android:layout_width="wrap_content"
       android:layout_height="wrap_content"
       android:textSize="56sp"
       app:layout_constraintBottom_toBottomOf="parent"
       app:layout_constraintLeft_toLeftOf="parent"
       app:layout_constraintRight_toRightOf="parent"
   ```

```xml
        app:layout_constraintTop_toTopOf="parent" />

    <Button
        android:id="@+id/cancel_btn"
        android:layout_width="wrap_content"
        android:layout_height="wrap_content"
        android:text="Cancel"
        app:layout_constraintBottom_toBottomOf="parent"
        app:layout_constraintLeft_toLeftOf="parent"
        app:layout_constraintRight_toRightOf="parent"/>

</androidx.constraintlayout.widget.ConstraintLayout>
```

3. Set the layout for `MainActivity` inside the `onCreate()` hook function:

```kotlin
class MainActivity : AppCompatActivity() {
    override fun onCreate(savedInstanceState: Bundle?) {
        super.onCreate(savedInstanceState)
        setContentView(R.layout.activity_main)
    }
}
```

4. Start a new coroutine running in the background, incrementing the counter every second and displaying it in the `TextView` obtained from the XML layout:

```kotlin
class MainActivity: AppCompatActivity() {
    override fun onCreate(savedInstanceState: Bundle?) {
        super.onCreate(savedInstanceState)
        setContentView(R.layout.activity_main)
        val job = launch {
            var counter = 1
            while (true) {
                delay(1000)
                counter++
                withContext(UI) {
                    text_field.text = counter.toString()
                }
            }
        }
    }
}
```

5. Allow coroutine-cancellation by clicking the **cancel** button:

```kotlin
class MainActivity: AppCompatActivity() {

    override fun onCreate(savedInstanceState: Bundle?) {
        super.onCreate(savedInstanceState)
```

```
        setContentView(R.layout.activity_main)
        text_field.text = "Bonjour!"

    val job = launch {
        var counter = 1
        while (true) {
            delay(1000)
            counter++
            withContext(UI) {
                text_field.text = counter.toString()
            }
        }
    }

    cancel_btn.setOnClickListener {
        job.cancel()
    }
  }
}
```

How it works...

The coroutine started in the `MainActivity.onCreate()` function is running an infinite `while` loop. Each iteration starts with a one-minute delay and incrementation of the counter variable. Next, we are applying the `withContext()` function in order to update `TextView` with the new value.

 The `withContext()` function allows us to switch to a new coroutine dispatcher, obtained from the context argument, in order to execute a block of code passed to it. It doesn't create and start a new coroutine, but it modifies the context of the parent coroutine immediately. The new dispatcher is applied only temporarily to execute a given block of code. Any further operations executed inside the coroutine scope after the `withContext()` function call will be run with the original coroutine context.

We are assigning a `Job` instance returned by the coroutine to the `job` variable. Next, we are setting up the listener to the cancel button. Whenever the cancel button is clicked, the `cancel()` function is invoked on the coroutine `Job` reference.

As the result, our `MainActivity` implementation is going to update the `TextView` value every second. Once the cancel button is clicked, the update mechanism is stopped immediately.

There's more...

If you're developing an application using different JVM frameworks, in order to switch to the UI thread from the background, you can use the `withContext()` function with the `JavaFx` or `Swing` constants instead of the Android `UI` context constants.

See also

- If you'd like to explore the basics of the coroutines framework, you should take a look at the recipes in `Chapter 7`, *Making Asynchronous Programming Great Again*

Easy class serialization on Android using the @Parcelize annotation

In this recipe, we are going to make use of the `@Parcelize` annotation to simplify the implementation of the Android `Parcelable` interface, allowing us to serialize objects efficiently. `@Parcelize` is available in the Kotlin Android Extensions plugin and provides automatic code-generation for Kotlin classes that implement the `Parcelable` interface.

Getting ready

We are going to implement the Android instrumented test case in order to verify the effect of a class serialization and deserialization in action. To make use of the Android KTX library, we need to add it to the project dependencies. In our case, we will need it in the `android-test` module. We can add it with the following declaration:

```
androidTestImplementation 'androidx.core:core-ktx:1.0.+'
```

In order to make use of the Kotlin Android Extensions plugin, we need to enable it in the Android project module-level `build.gradle` script by adding the following declaration:

```
apply plugin: 'kotlin-android-extensions'
```

You can examine the implementation and configuration of recipes related to the Android framework in the AndroidSamples project available in the book's GitHub repository: https://github.com/PacktPublishing/Kotlin-Standard-Library-Cookbook/ . To follow Android-related recipes, you just need to create a new project in Android Studio.

How to do it...

1. Let's start by creating a sample User class that implements the `Parcelable` interface using the `@Parcelize` annotation:

```
@Parcelize
data class User(val name: String, val address: Address): Parcelable

@Parcelize
data class Address(val street: String,
                   val number: String,
                   val city: String): Parcelable
```

2. Verify serialization and deserialization of the `User` class instance by writing and reading it from the `Bundle` instance:

```
@Test
fun testUserParcelisation() {
    // given
    val originalUser = User("Bob", Address("Rue de Paris", "123",
      "Warsaw"))
    val bundle = Bundle()

    // when
    bundle.putParcelable("my_user", originalUser)

    // then
    val deserialisedUser = bundle.get("my_user") as User
    assertEquals(originalUser, deserialisedUser)
}
```

How it works...

We have started by defining the User class, which contains a property of the Address class. Both User and Address are decorated with the @Parcelize annotation. It tells the Android Extensions plugin to generate code for the Parcelable interface implementation. Inside the testUserParcelisation() function, we are creating an instance of the User class and serializing it using the Android Bundle mechanism. We are putting the original User class instance to the Bundle under the "my_user" key, and later we deserialize its instance by calling bundle.get("my_user") as User. Finally, we compare the original and deserialized User instances using the assertEquals() function.

@Parcelize handles generating the Parcelable implementation for the following types:

All the primitive types, String, CharSequence, objects and enums, Exception, Size, SizeF, Bundle, IBinder, IInterface, FileDescriptor, SparseArray, SparseIntArray, SparseLongArray, and SparseBooleanArray. It also supports any Serializable types (for example, java.util.Date), as well as Collection and Array types. It also works with nullable types.

See also

- You can learn more about the features dedicated to Android development in the Kotlin Android Extensions plugin by studying the official guide: https://kotlinlang.org/docs/tutorials/android-plugin.html

Implementing a custom property delegate that provides lifecycle-aware values

Often, we need to declare a class property, which should depend on the lifecycle state of Activity or Fragment. In this recipe, we are going to employ both the Kotlin Lazy delegate and the Lifecycle class provided by the Android Architecture Components library (https://developer.android.com/topic/libraries/architecture/). We are going to implement a custom property delegate that will provide values in a lazy manner. This means that they are going to be instantiated only on the first call. Moreover, we are going to clear their values once Activity or Fragment gets destroyed. This will avoid memory leaks, which can be caused by managing properties dependent on the Context instance with the standard Lazy delegate.

Getting ready

The basic Lazy delegate initialized using the lazy() function provided by the standard library gives the desired possibility of declaring a property of a non-null type, which can only be instantiated after a certain lifecycle event. For example, we reference an element of a screen layout in a property only after the layout was set up inside the Activity.onCreate() hook function.

However, such an implementation using `Lazy` will cause a memory leak if the property holds a reference to the `Activity` instance internally, as it will not allow it to be deleted by a garbage collector. The reason for this is that the lazy delegate is caching the instance it's holding. We are going to implement our own property delegate, called `LifeCycleAwareLazy`, which will both extend the `Lazy` interface and clear the value it's holding when the activity is about to be destroyed.

We are going to use the `Lifecycle` library module available with the Android Architecture Components provided by Google. We need to add it to the project dependencies in the module-level `build.gradle` script:

```
implementation "android.arch.lifecycle:runtime:1.1.1"
```

How to do it...

1. Declare the `LifecycleAwareLazy` class:

   ```
   class LifecycleAwareLazy<T>(lifecycle: Lifecycle, val initializer:
   () -> T) :            Lazy<T>, GenericLifecycleObserver
   ```

2. Register an observer to the given `Lifecycle` instance inside the `init` block:

   ```
   class LifecycleAwareLazy<T>(lifecycle: Lifecycle, val initializer:
   () -> T) :            Lazy<T>, GenericLifecycleObserver {
       init {
           lifecycle.addObserver(this)
       }
   }
   ```

3. Implement an internal field that represents the current value stored by the delegate:

   ```
   class LifecycleAwareLazy<T>(lifecycle: Lifecycle, val initializer:
   () -> T) :            Lazy<T>, GenericLifecycleObserver {

       init {
           lifecycle.addObserver(this)
       }
       private object UNINITIALIZED_VALUE
       private var _value: Any? = UNINITIALIZED_VALUE
   }
   ```

4. Implement the `value` property and the `isInitialized()` function required by the `Lazy` interface:

```
class LifecycleAwareLazy<T>(lifecycle: Lifecycle, val initializer:
() -> T): Lazy<T>, GenericLifecycleObserver {

    init {
        lifecycle.addObserver(this)
    }

    private object UNINITIALIZED_VALUE
    private var _value: Any? = UNINITIALIZED_VALUE

    @get:Synchronized
    override val value: T
        get() {
            if (_value === UNINITIALIZED_VALUE) {
                _value = initializer.invoke()
            }
            return _value as T
        }

    override fun isInitialized(): Boolean = _value !=
UNINITIALIZED_VALUE
}
```

5. Implement the `GenericLifecycleObserver` interface:

```
class LifecycleAwareLazy<T>(lifecycle: Lifecycle, val initializer:
() -> T): Lazy<T>, GenericLifecycleObserver {

    init {
        lifecycle.addObserver(this)
    }

    private object UNINITIALIZED_VALUE
    private var _value: Any? = UNINITIALIZED_VALUE

    @get:Synchronized
    override val value: T
        get() {
            if (_value === UNINITIALIZED_VALUE) {
                _value = initializer.invoke()
            }
            return _value as T
        }

    override fun isInitialized(): Boolean = _value !=
```

```
UNINITIALIZED_VALUE

    override fun onStateChanged(source: LifecycleOwner?, event:
Lifecycle.Event?) {
        when (event) {
            Lifecycle.Event.ON_STOP -> {
                _value = UNINITIALIZED_VALUE
            }
            else -> return
        }
    }
}
```

How it works...

The `LifecycleAwareLazy` class we have implemented can be seen as an extended version of the standard `Lazy` delegate implementation. It observes events emitted by the `Lifecycle` instance passed to it in the constructor and handles the value accordingly. Internally, it contains the private `_value: Any?` mutable property set initially to the `UNINITIALIZED_VALUE` object, which represents an empty state. The `_value` property reflects the current state of the delegated property, which can be initialized or uninitialized. The `LifecycleAwareLazy` class exposes also the immutable `value` property, which is responsible for returning a final value of the delegated property. Not it is marked with the `@get:Synchronized` annotation which informs the compiler to generate thread-safe getter function for this property.

Inside the `value` property getter, the current value of the `_value` property is checked. Whenever it is equal to `UNINITIALIZED_VALUE`, first it gets reassigned to the result of the `initialiser` function passed in the constructor and then it is returned as the value of the delegated property.

 `Lifecycle` is a class that holds the information about the current lifecycle state of an associated component (such as an activity or a fragment). It allows other objects to observe this state by subscribing to the state-change events by passing a callback to the `Lifecycle.addObserver()` function. You can also obtain a current state by accessing the `Lifecycle.currentState` property.

Inside the `init` block, we are subscribing to the state updates of the `Lifecycle` object passed as the `LifecycleAwareLazy` constructor parameter. We are passing the `LifecycleAwareLazy` instance using the `GenericLifecycleObserver` implementation to the `lifecycle.addObserver(this)` function.

We implement the `GenericLifeObserver` interface by overriding the `onStateChanged()` function inside the `LifecycleAwareLazy` class. As you can see, we are updating the `_value` mutable property to the `UNINITIALIZED_VALUE` object whenever the `Lifecycle.Event.ON_STOP` event is emitted, meaning that the activity is about to be destroyed. This way, we can be sure that the `_value` property won't block the activity or fragment from being garbage-collected, even if it holds a reference to an activity `Context` instance directly or indirectly. This is a huge win compared to the standard lazy delegate, which can lead to potential memory leaks.

See also

- If you'd like to get familiar with the basics of the property-delegation pattern, take a look at the *Implementing delegated class properties* recipe from `Chapter 5`, *Tasteful Design Patterns Adopting Kotlin Concepts*

Easy operations on SharedPreferences

In this recipe, we will make use of the Android KTX library developed by Google, providing a set of useful extensions and utilities dedicated to Android app-development. We are going to apply extension functions that allow us to operate on the `SharedPreferences` class in a clean and robust way.

Getting ready

In order to make use of the Android KTX library, we need to add it to the project dependencies. In our case, we will need it in the `android-test` module. We can add it with the following declaration:

```
androidTestImplementation 'androidx.core:core-ktx:1.0.+'
```

We are going to implement the Android instrumented test case in order to verify the effects of the operations we'll perform on `SharedPreferences`. You can examine the implementation and configuration of recipes related to the Android framework in the AndroidSamples project available in the GitHub repository: `https://github.com/PacktPublishing/Kotlin-Standard-Library-Cookbook/`. To follow Android-related recipes, you just need to create a new project in Android Studio.

How to do it...

1. Create a function that returns the `SharedPreferences` instance:

```
fun getDefaultSharedPreferences() =
PreferenceManager.getDefaultSharedPreferences(InstrumentationRegist
ry.getContext())
```

2. Save a sample string to the `SharedPreferences` instance:

```
@Test
fun testUserParcelization() {
    val prefs = getDefaultSharedPreferences()
    val userName: String = "Gonzo"
    prefs.edit {
        putString("user_name", userName)
    }
}
```

3. Verify whether the string was successfully saved:

```
@Test
fun testSharedPrefs() {
    val prefs = getDefaultSharedPreferences()
    val userName: String = "Gonzo"
    prefs.edit {
        putString("user_name", userName)
    }

    val DEFAULT_VALUE = "empty"
    val fetchedUserName = prefs.getString("user_name",
     DEFAULT_VALUE)
    assertSame(userName, fetchedUserName)
}
```

How it works...

We are using the `edit()` extension function provided by the KTX library for the `SharedPreferences` class. It takes the lambda block, including the operations we want to perform on the `SharedPreferences.Editor` instance, and automatically invokes the `SharedPreferences.Editor.apply()` function to submit the transaction. The lambda block passed to the `edit()` function implements the type, `SharedPreferences.Editor.() -> Unit`, which allows us to access an instance of `Editor` through the implicit `this` modifier.

If you'd like to submit operations applied to the Editor using the blocking commit() instead of the asynchronous apply() function, you should pass an additional commit = true parameter to the edit() function.

See also

- If you'd like to get familiar with more features offered by the Android KTX library, take a look at the library's official guide: https://developer.android.com/kotlin/ktx

Less boilerplate Cursor data parsing

In this recipe, we are going to learn how to work with the Android Cursor type in a more effective and easy way. We are going to create an extension function for the Cursor type, allowing us to query it in a clean way. We will also implement a practical example showing how to access the system-content resolver in order to fetch contacts stored on the device and transform Cursor into a list of strings representing the contacts' names.

Getting ready

You can examine the implementation and configuration of the recipes related to the Android framework in the AndroidSamples project available in the GitHub repository: https://github.com/PacktPublishing/Kotlin-Standard-Library-Cookbook/. To follow Android-related recipes, you just need to create a new project in Android Studio.

How to do it...

1. Implement an extension function that allows us to fetch the values of a requested column name from Cursor:

```
fun Cursor.getString(columnName: String): String? {
    return getString(getColumnIndex(columnName))
}
```

2. Obtain the `Cursor` instance that points to the system contacts table:

```
val NOT_SPECIFIED = ""
val content = getContext().contentResolver
val projection = arrayOf(ContactsContract.Data.DISPLAY_NAME)
val cursor =
        content.query(ContactsContract.Contacts.CONTENT_URI,
                projection,
                NOT_SPECIFIED,
                emptyArray(),
                NOT_SPECIFIED)
```

3. Invoke the `use` function on the `cursor` instance and iterate through the data inside its scope:

```
val NOT_SPECIFIED = ""
val content = getContext().contentResolver
val projection = arrayOf(ContactsContract.Data.DISPLAY_NAME)
val cursor =
        content.query(ContactsContract.Contacts.CONTENT_URI,
                projection,
                NOT_SPECIFIED,
                emptyArray(),
                NOT_SPECIFIED)

val contacts = cursor.use {
    val contactsList = mutableListOf<String?>()
    while (it.moveToNext()) {
        val contactName =
it.getString(ContactsContract.Data.DISPLAY_NAME)
        contactsList.add(contactName)
    }
    contactsList
}
```

How it works...

We are applying the `use()` extension function provided by the standard library to execute a set of operations on the `Cursor` instance. `use()` can be invoked on any class that implements the `Closeable` interface. Internally, after executing the lambda block passed to it as an argument, `use()` automatically invokes the `close()` function on the object it was called on. Thanks to that, we can safely perform any operation on the `Cursor` instance and be sure that, even if some of them fail or result in throwing an exception, the cursor will eventually be closed.

Inside the `use()` function's scope, we are iterating the cursor with the `while` loop by moving it to the next row in each iteration. For each of the rows, we are using the `getString()` extension function to obtain the current contact display name from the cursor. It allows us to avoid code duplication by combining `Cursor.getString()` and `Cursor.getColumnIndex()` together.

Mocking dependencies with the Mockito Kotlin library

Often when writing unit test cases for complex classes, we face the problem of instantiating a great number of properties that the class we want to test depends on. Although this problem could be solved with dependency injection, it is faster, more efficient, and more desirable to mock a behavior of a specific object without instantiating it at all. In this recipe, we are going to explore how to use the Mockito Kotlin library to mock dependencies when writing a unit test for a simple registration form that contains an internal dependency whose behavior we are going to mock.

Getting ready

We are going to use the JUnit library, which provides the core framework for running test-case classes. We need to add it our project's list of project dependencies by declaring it in the `gradle.build` script:

```
implementation group: 'junit', name: 'junit', version: '4.12'
```

In order to make use of the Kotlin Mockito library, we can add it to the project dependencies with the following declaration:

```
implementation 'com.nhaarman:mockito-kotlin:1.5.0'
```

You can examine the implementation and configuration of the recipes related to the Android framework in the AndroidSamples project available in the GitHub repository: `https://github.com/PacktPublishing/Kotlin-Standard-Library-Cookbook/`. To follow Android-related recipes, you just need to create a new project in Android Studio.

In this recipe, we are going to write a unit test for the `RegistrationFormController` class, declared as follows:

```
class RegistrationFormController(val api: RegistrationApi) {
    var currentEmailAddress: String = ""

    fun isEmailValid(): Boolean = currentEmailAddress.contains("@")

    fun checkIfEmailCanBeRegistered(): Boolean =
        isEmailIsValid() &&
api.isEmailAddressAvailable(currentEmailAddress)
}
```

`RegistrationApi` is defined as the following interface:

```
interface RegistrationApi {
    fun isEmailAddressAvailable(email: String): Boolean
}
```

Since we don't want to implement the `RegistrationApi` interface in order to instantiate the `RegistrationFormController` class, we are going to mock it instead using the Mockito Kotlin `mock()` function.

How to do it...

1. Create a new test class:

    ```
    class MyTest {
    }
    ```

2. Create a mocked instance of the `RegistrationApi` interface as the test-class property:

    ```
    class MyTest {
        private val api = mock<RegistrationApi>()
    }
    ```

3. Add a class property of the `RegistrationFormController` type:

    ```
    class MyTest {
        private val api = mock<RegistrationApi>()
        private var registrationFormController =
            RegistrationFormController(api = api)
    }
    ```

4. Create the test method to check whether `checkIfEmailCanBeRegistered()` behaves correctly for an invalid email address occurrence:

```
class MyTest {
    private val api = mock<RegistrationApi>()
    private lateinit var registrationFormController:
RegistrationFormController

    @Before
    fun setup() {
        registrationFormController = RegistrationFormController(api
= api)
    }

    @Test
    fun `email shouldn't be registered if it's not valid`() {
        // given
        assertNotNull(registrationFormController)
        whenever(api.isEmailAddressAvailable(anyString()))
doReturn(true)
        // when
        registrationFormController.currentEmailAddress = "Hilary"
        // then
assertFalse(registrationFormController.checkIfEmailCanBeRegistered(
))
    }
}
```

How it works...

Inside the `email shouldn't be registered if it's not valid`() test method, we are setting up our mocked `RegistrationApi` property to return `true` any time its `isEmailAddressAvailable()` function is invoked, regardless of the string value passed to it. Next, we are updating the `currentEmailAddress` property of the `RegistrationFormController` class with an invalid email address value. The test is going to pass because the `isEmailIsValid()` function works correctly and returns `false` for a given email address value.

As you can see, thanks to the mocking, we've avoided implementing the dependency of the class we were testing. It's a proper technique that allows us to test the specific parts of the business logic while mimicking the desired behavior of the dependencies. Mocking can be also useful when we are not able to instantiate the dependencies because they are specific to a platform that is not compatible with the pure JVM (that is, Android).

See also

- You can look into the *Verifying function invocations* recipe in order to explore how to check whether any specific interactions with the mocked dependency were observed

Verifying function invocations

Along with the possibility of simulating the particular behavior of dependencies in test methods, mocking allows us to verify whether specific functions of the mocked objects were invoked. In this recipe, we are going to write a unit tests for a simple registration-form controller. The registration form contains two internal dependencies that we are going to mock using the Mockito Kotlin library. We are going to test whether the proper functions are being invoked in different scenarios.

Getting ready

We are going to use the JUnit library to provide a core framework for running test-case classes. We need to add it to our project's list of project dependencies by declaring it in the `gradle.build` script:

```
implementation group: 'junit', name: 'junit', version: '4.12'
```

In order to make use of the Kotlin Mockito library, we can add it to the project dependencies with the following declaration:

```
implementation 'com.nhaarman:mockito-kotlin:1.5.0'
```

You can examine the implementation and configuration of recipes related to the Android framework in the AndroidSamples project available in the GitHub repository: `https://github.com/PacktPublishing/Kotlin-Standard-Library-Cookbook/`. To follow Android-related recipes, you just need to create a new project in Android Studio.

In this recipe, we are going to write a unit test for the `RegistrationFormController` class, declared as follows:

```
class RegistrationForm(val api: RegistrationApi, val view: TextView) {
    var currentEmailAddress: String by
        Delegates.observable("", ::onEmailAddressNewValue)

    fun onEmailAddressNewValue(prop: KProperty<*>, old: String,
     new: String) {
        if (checkIfEmailCanBeRegistered()) {
            view.showSuccessMessage("Email address is available!")
        } else {
            view.showErrorMessage("This email address is not
              available.")
        }
    }

    fun checkIfEmailCanBeRegistered(): Boolean =
            isEmailIsValid() &&
    api.isEmailAddressAvailable(currentEmailAddress)

    fun isEmailIsValid(): Boolean = currentEmailAddress.contains("@")

}
```

It contains the `RegistrationApi` property which is defined as the following interface:

```
interface RegistrationApi {
    fun isEmailAddressAvailable(email: String): Boolean
}
```

and the `TextView` type property defined as follows:

```
interface TextView {
    fun showSuccessMessage(message: String)
    fun showErrorMessage(message: String)
}
```

Since we don't want to implement the `RegistrationApi` and `TextView` interface in order to instantiate the `RegistrationFormController` class in our test, we are going to mock them using the Mockito Kotlin `mock()` function.

How to do it...

1. Create a new test class:

```
class MyTest {
}
```

2. Create a mocked instance of the RegistrationApi interface as the test-class property:

```
class MyTest {
    private val api = mock<RegistrationApi>()
}
```

3. Create a mocked TextView instance:

```
class MyTest {
    private val api = mock<RegistrationApi>()
    private val view = mock<TextView>()
}
```

4. Create the RegistrationFormController object as the MyTest class property:

```
class MyTest {
    private val api = mock<RegistrationApi>()
    private val view = mock<TextView>()
    private var registrationForm = RegistrationForm(api, view)
}
```

5. Add a test method to verify whether the success message is shown if the address is available:

```
class MyTest {
    private val api = mock<RegistrationApi>()
    private val view = mock<TextView>()
    private var registrationForm = RegistrationForm(api, view)

    @Test
    fun `should display success message when email address is
available`() {
        // given
        assertNotNull(registrationForm)
        // when we update the currentEmailAddress to any String
whenever(api.isEmailAddressAvailable(ArgumentMatchers.anyString()))
doReturn(true)
        registrationForm.currentEmailAddress = "hilary@gmail.com"
        // then
```

```
        assertTrue(registrationForm.checkIfEmailCanBeRegistered())
        verify(view).showSuccessMessage("Email address is
         available!")
    }
}
```

6. Add a test method to verify whether the error message is shown if the address is not available:

```
class MyTest {
    private val api = mock<RegistrationApi>()
    private val view = mock<TextView>()
    private var registrationForm = RegistrationForm(api, view)

    @Test
    fun `should display success message when email address is
available`() {
        // given
        assertNotNull(registrationForm)
        // when we update the currentEmailAddress to any String
whenever(api.isEmailAddressAvailable(ArgumentMatchers.anyString()))
doReturn(true)
        registrationForm.currentEmailAddress = "hilary@gmail.com"
        // then
        assertTrue(registrationForm.checkIfEmailCanBeRegistered())
        verify(view).showSuccessMessage("Email address is
available!")
    }

    @Test
    fun `should display error message when email address isn't
available`() {
        // given
        assertNotNull(registrationForm)
        // when
        registrationForm.currentEmailAddress = "hilary@gmail.com"
whenever(api.isEmailAddressAvailable(ArgumentMatchers.anyString()))
doReturn(false)
        // then
        assertTrue(registrationForm.isEmailIsValid())
        verify(view).showErrorMessage(anyString())
    }
}
```

How it works...

Apart from behavior-mocking, Mockito Kotlin provides a reliable way of verifying interactions with mocked dependencies that occurred while executing the test method. In both the `should display success message when email address is available`() and `should display error message when email address isn't available`() functions, we just want to check whether the desired function of the `TextView` dependency was invoked. In order to do this, we are invoking the `verify()` function. For example, in order to check whether the `showErrorMessage()` function has been called on the mocked `view: TextView` dependency, we call the following code:

```
verify(view).showErrorMessage(anyString())
```

If the `showErrorMessage()` is not invoked, the test method will fail and the proper log message will be printed to the console.

Unit tests for Kotlin coroutines

In this recipe, we are going to explore how to effectively test code that uses coroutines internally. We are going to write a unit test for the part of a code that runs asynchronously in the background while trying to authorize the given user credentials using an external API. We are going to employ the Kotlin Mockito library to mock the calls to the external API and the `TextCoroutineContext` class, allowing us to test asynchronous code with ease.

Getting ready

We are going to use the JUnit library to provide the core framework for running test-case classes. We need to add it to our project's list of project dependencies by declaring it in the `gradle.build` script:

```
implementation group: 'junit', name: 'junit', version: '4.12'
```

In order to make use of the Kotlin Mockito library, we can add it to the project dependencies with the following declaration:

```
implementation 'com.nhaarman:mockito-kotlin:1.5.0'
```

You can examine the implementation and configuration of recipes related to the Android framework in the AndroidSamples project available in the GitHub repository: `https://github.com/PacktPublishing/Kotlin-Standard-Library-Cookbook/`. To follow Android-related recipes, you just need to create a new project in Android Studio.

In this recipe, we are going to write a unit test for the `Authenticator` class, defined as follows:

```
class Authenticator(val api: Api) {

    fun tryToAuthorise(encodedUserNameAndPassword: ByteArray,
                       context: CoroutineContext): Deferred<String> =
        async(context) {
            var authToken = api.authorise(encodedUserNameAndPassword)

            var retryCount = 0
            while (authToken.isEmpty() && retryCount <= 8) {
                delay(10, TimeUnit.SECONDS)
                authToken = api.authorise(encodedUserNameAndPassword)
                retryCount++
            }

            authToken
        }
}
```

The `Api` property is given as the following interface:

```
interface Api {
    // returns a non-empty auth token when the given credentials were
    authorised
    fun authorise(encodedUserNameAndPassword: ByteArray): String
}
```

How to do it...

1. Create a new test class:

    ```
    class MyTest {
    }
    ```

2. Add a mocked `Api` type test-class property:

```
class MyTest {
    val api: Api = mock()
}
```

3. Instantiate the `Authenticator` class as the class property:

```
class MyTest {
    val api: Api = mock()
    val authenticator = Authenticator(api)
}
```

4. Implement the test to verify whether the `Api.authorise()` function is called at least 10 times in case of consecutive failed authorization attempts:

```
class MyTest {
    val api: Api = mock()
    val authenticator = Authenticator(api)

    @Test
    fun `should retry auth at least 10 times when Api returns empty
    token`() {
        whenever(api.authorise(any())) doReturn ""

        val context = TestCoroutineContext()

        runBlocking(context) {
          authenticator.tryToAuthorise("admin:1234".toByteArray(),
            context)
                    .await()
          context.advanceTimeBy(100, TimeUnit.SECONDS)
          verify(api, atLeast(10)).authorise(any())
        }
    }
}
```

How it works...

First, with mocking, we've avoided implementing the `Api` dependency of the `Authenticator` class we were writing the test for. In fact, we are not interested in testing real results returned by the `Api` implementation. We want to test the mechanism of the `tryToAuthorise()` function and verify whether it's going to retry calling the `Api.authorise()` function at least 10 times in case of constant authorization failures. This is why we have set up the `api` mock to always return an empty string for the `authorise()` function result.

As you can imagine, such a test would take a lot of time to complete because, internally, the `tryToAuthorise()` function waits for 10 seconds before retrying the authorization. In order to avoid the too-long execution time, we need to artificially move forward in time by 100 seconds and check whether the `Api.authorise()` function was invoked at least 10 times. We are able to do this by scheduling the two coroutines started with the `runBlocking()` function, and internally inside the `tryToAuthorise()` function, to run on the same instance of `TestCoroutineContext`. Then, to move forward in time by 100 seconds, we just call the `advanceTimeBy(100, TimeUnit.SECONDS)` function on the `TestCoroutineContext` instance. As a result, our test method is going to complete in less than a second.

9
Miscellaneous

In this chapter, we will cover the following recipes:

- Kotlin and Java interoperability issues
- Kotlin and JavaScript interoperability issues
- Renaming of generated classes
- Decompiling Kotlin code to JVM bytecode
- Adding custom names for imports
- Wrapping complex type declarations with type aliases
- Expressive `try...catch` declarations
- Safe type-casting

Introduction

This chapter is going to focus on presenting handy solutions to various problems and issues that Kotlin developers deal with on a daily basis. Here, you will find useful tips and solutions for issues related to interoperability with Java and JavaScript and neat tricks that will help you write code more effectively.

Kotlin and Java interoperability

This recipe is going to show how you to combine both Java and Kotlin classes together and use them in the same application component. We will declare a Kotlin data class, called `ColoredText`, that holds two properties of the `String` and `Color` types. Apart from the properties, it is also going to expose a utility function inside a companion object responsible for text-processing. We are going to learn how to make use of those properties and how to declare the function from the `ColoredText` class to be visible as a JVM static method inside the Java class.

How to do it...

1. Declare the `ColoredText` class:

```
data class ColoredText
@JvmOverloads
constructor(
        var text: String = "",
        var color: Color = defaultColor) {

    companion object {
        @JvmField
        val defaultColor = Color.BLUE
    }
}
```

2. Implement a static JVM method inside the `companion` object:

```
data class ColoredText
@JvmOverloads
constructor(
        var text: String = "",
        var color: Color = defaultColor) {

    companion object {
        @JvmField
        val defaultColor = Color.BLUE

        @JvmStatic
        fun processText(text: String): String =
                with(text) {
                    toLowerCase().trim().capitalize()
                }

    }

}
```

3. Add a member function that enables you to print the `text` property to the console:

```
data class ColoredText
@JvmOverloads
constructor(
        var text: String = "",
        var color: Color = defaultColor) {
```

```kotlin
fun printToConsole() = println(text)

companion object {
    @JvmField
    val defaultColor = Color.BLUE

    @JvmStatic
    fun processText(text: String): String =
            with(text) {
                toLowerCase().trim().capitalize()
            }
    }
}
```

4. Implement a Java class that makes use of Kotlin class functions and properties:

```java
public class JavaApp {
    public static void main(String... args) {
        String rawText =
            " one Of The Best Programming Skills You Can Have " +
            "Is Knowing When To Walk Away For Awhile. ";
        String text = ColoredText.processText(rawText);
        ColoredText myText = new ColoredText(text,
         ColoredText.defaultColor);
        myText.printToConsole();
    }
}
```

How it works...

As the result, the main function from the `JavaApp` Java class is going to print the following wisdom to the console:

```
One of the best programming skills you can have is knowing when to walk
away for awhile.
```

Kotlin and Java interoperability is absolutely painless, thanks to the fact that both Kotlin and Java classes are compiled to the same JVM bytecode included in a common codebase. However, there are a few special cases that require additional attention when we want to make Kotlin declarations available on the Java side in a specific way.

First of all, in the `ColoredText` class, we are marking the constructor with the `@JvmOverloads` annotation, which tells the compiler to generate multiple instances of the constructor in case there are any default property values declared. Thanks to this, we could instantiate the `ColoredText` class in some Java classes without passing the `text` and/or `color` property values.

Next annotation we are using is `@JvmField`, which tells the Kotlin compiler not to generate getter and setter functions for this property and expose it as a field. It provides a cleaner syntax for accessing the values on the Java side when we expose a constant value through Kotlin objects.

Another commonly used annotation is `@JvmStatic`. Its aim is to tell the compiler that an additional static method needs to be generated for this function in order to make it available in Java as a direct static function of the outer class. For example, in our case, we are able to access the `processText()` function in Java in the following manner, by omitting the `Companion` element:

```
ColoredText.processText("sample text")
```

Kotlin and JavaScript interoperability

In the following recipe, we are going to configure and implement a sample web app project in order to explore how Kotlin can be compiled to JavaScript. We are going to implement a simple web app that will open an alert dialog when the app starts. The following example is going to present a way of combining Kotlin and JavaScript code together and configuring a JavaScript compilation with the Gradle build script.

Getting ready

In order to set up the project to compile Kotlin files into JavaScript, we need to add the following properties to the module-level Gradle build script. First, we need to apply the Kotlin2Js plugin. We can do it with the following declaration:

```
apply plugin: "kotlin2js"
```

At this point, whenever we execute the Gradle `build` task, the Kotlin2JS compiler is going to generate JavaScript code with the corresponding functions and classes from the Kotlin files and write them under the `build/classes/kotlin/` directory to the JS file named after the project name. However, we can modify this default behavior by specifying the output file parameter:

```
compileKotlin2Js.kotlinOptions.outputFile = "${projectDir}/web/js/app.js"
```

As the result, the output of the Kotlin files' compilation will be available under `web/js` directory, in the `app.js` file.

However, in order to execute the translated Kotlin code, we need to link the Kotlin JS standard library to it as well. We can modify the Gradle build script to include the required libraries in the `web/js` output directory:

```
build.doLast {
    configurations.compile.each { File file ->
        copy {
            includeEmptyDirs = false

            from zipTree(file.absolutePath)
            into "${projectDir}/web/js/lib"
            include { fileTreeElement ->
                def path = fileTreeElement.path
                path.endsWith(".js") && (path.startsWith("META-
INF/resources/") || !path.startsWith("META-INF/"))
            }
        }
    }
}
```

You can examine the configuration of the Kotlin2JS plugin in the sample project: `https://github.com/PacktPublishing/Kotlin-Standard-Library-Cookbook/tree/master/Kotlin-Samples-JS`.

How to do it...

1. Create a new kotlin file, `AlertDialogApp.kt`, that contains the `main()` function:

```
fun main(args : Array<String>) {}
```

2. Declare a reference to the JS `alert()` function:

```
fun main(args : Array<String>) {}

external fun alert(message: Any?): Unit
```

3. Implement the `showAlert()` function and invoke it in the `main()` function:

```
fun main(args : Array<String>) {
    showAlert()
}

fun showAlert() {
    val number: dynamic = js("Math.floor(Math.random() * 1000)")
    val message = "There were $number viruses found on your
computer! \uD83D\uDE31"
    println("showing alert")
    alert(message)
}

external fun alert(message: Any?): Unit
```

How it works...

As you can see, after running the Gradle build task, the `AlertDialogApp.kt` file is going to be translated into the `app.js` JavaScript code, available under the `web/js` directory, along with the `kotlin.js` file linked under the `web/js/lib` directory.

We can test the JS-generated code by running it in the web browser. In order to do so, we will create a sample HTML file under the project's main directory, named `test_app.html`, which is going to link the `kotlin.js` standard library file and run the `app.js` file that contains the `main()` function implementation generated from the `AlertDialogApp.kt` file:

```html
<!DOCTYPE html>
<html lang="en">
<head>
    <meta charset="UTF-8">
    <title>Test</title>
</head>
<body>
    <script src="web/js/lib/kotlin.js"></script>
    <script src="web/js/app.js"></script>
</body>
</html>
```

As the result, when we open the `test_app.html` file in a web browser, we are going to encounter the following pop-up dialog:

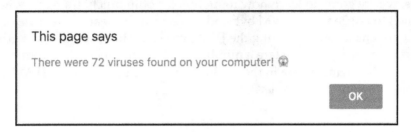

Inside the `showAlert()` function in the `AlertDialogApp.kt` file, we are using the JavaScript `Math.floor()` and `Math.random()` functions to generate a random integer value from 0-1,000. We are using the `js()` function available in the Kotlin standard library to inline JS code in the Kotlin code. As you can see, the result returned by `js()` is declared as a `dynamic` type.

> The `dynamic` modifier is used to declare the dynamic type, which is characteristic for every JavaScript object. In Kotlin code, it can be used as an alternative to strongly-typed declarations. It makes sense to use it whenever we are dealing with third-party JS libraries that can return the results of not-specified types.

Next, we are using the random integer value generated using the JS-inlined code to compose the message that is going to be displayed. Finally, we are calling the JS `alert()` function and passing it the composed message. This time, we are using the `external` modifier, which tells the Kotlin compiler that the corresponding declaration is written in pure JavaScript and it should not generate the implementation for it.

There's more...

You may wonder whether there is a practical solution to working with npm JS dependencies within a Gradle-based project. There is a solution that allows you to integrate your Kotlin project with npm dependencies easily, called the Kotlin Frontend Gradle plugin. You can learn more about it in the official project guide: `https://github.com/Kotlin/kotlin-frontend-plugin`.

Renaming generated functions

In this recipe, we are going to learn how to modify a Kotlin function's name when it is being compiled to the generated JVM bytecode. We need this feature because of the type-erasure that happens when generating the JVM bytecode. However, thanks to the @JvmName annotation, we can declare a number of different functions, but that has the same name and use their original name in the Kotlin code while keeping their JVM bytecode names distinct to satisfy the compiler.

How to do it...

1. Declare two functions that have the same names:

```kotlin
fun List<String>.join(): String {
    return joinToString()
}

fun List<Int>.join(): String =
    map { it.toString() }
            .joinToString()
```

2. Mark the functions with the proper annotations:

```kotlin
@JvmName("joinStringList")
fun List<String>.join(): String {
    return joinToString()
}

@JvmName("joinIntList")
fun List<Int>.join(): String =
    map { it.toString() }
            .joinToString()
```

How it works...

Thanks to providing the alternative function names, we were able to compile them to JVM bytecode. However, you can easily test that we can use their original names inside the Kotlin code. That's because the Kotlin compiler is able to recognize them correctly based on their return type and generic type argument value.

You can test this by running the `join()` function both on the list of integers and on the list of strings:

```
fun main(vararg args: String) {
    println(listOf(1, 2, 3).join())
    println(listOf("a", "b", "c").join())
}
```

As the result, the preceding code will print the following text to the console:

```
1, 2, 3
a, b, c
```

Keep in mind that, when you want to invoke those functions from Java, you will need to use their alternative names: `joinStringList()` and `joinIntList()`.

There's more...

There is also a corresponding `@JsName` annotation, which allows you to change the name of JavaScript functions and classes. You can use it if you are compiling your Kotlin files to JavaScript using the Kotlin2JS plugin. If you'd like to get familiar with the basics of the Kotlin2JS plugin, you can examine the *Kotlin and JavaScript interoperability* recipe.

See also

- If you'd like to learn how to explore the final JVM bytecode generated from Kotlin files, read the *Decompiling Kotlin code to Java and JVM bytecode* recipe

Decompiling Kotlin code to Java and JVM bytecode

In this recipe, we are going to learn how to easily decompile our Kotlin files to see how their corresponding JVM bytecode is implemented and what the bytecode's corresponding Java implementation would look like. This can help you to discover how various Kotlin concepts were implemented under the hood. It can also be helpful for code-debugging and optimization.

Getting ready

Let's create a new Kotlin file, named `Recipe4.kt`, that contains the following sample implementation in order to see its bytecode translation:

```kotlin
data class A(val a: String = "a") {
    companion object {
        @JvmStatic
        fun foo(): String = "Wooo!"
    }
}
```

How to do it...

1. Open the `Recipe4.kt` file in IntelliJ.
2. Choose the **Show Kotlin Bytecode** option from the **Tools/Kotlin** menu. The box will present the JVM bytecode implementation.
3. Click the **Decompile** button in the **Kotlin Bytecode** view. The corresponding Java implementation will be decompiled from the bytecode and will appear in the new window.

How it works...

The task of analyzing the Java implementation generated for `data class A` is left as an exercise for the reader. You can experiment by removing the `data` modifier from the Kotlin class definition and observing the changes in the bytecode and the decompiled Java implementation.

Adding custom names for imports

In this recipe, we are going to explore how to add custom names to the `import` declarations. We are going to import the `java.lang.StringBuilder` class, add a custom name to it and make use of it in the sample code to demonstrate it in action.

How to do it...

1. Import the `StringBuilder` class with a custom alias:

```
import java.lang.StringBuilder as builder
```

2. Use the custom `StringBuilder` name in the sample code:

```
import java.lang.StringBuilder as builder

fun main(vararg args: String) {
    val text = builder()
            .append("Code is like humor. ")
            .append("When you have to explain it, ")
            .append("it's bad.")
            .toString()
    println(text)
}
```

How it works...

As you can see, we were able to use an alternative name instead of the `StringBuilder` class. It's a small feature but sometimes can be used to make your code easier to read. Our sample code is going to print the following text to the console:

```
Code is like humor. When you have to explain it, it's bad.
```

Wrapping complex type declarations with type aliases

Sometimes we need to deal with long or verbose type declarations. Thankfully, in Kotlin, we are able to assign an alternative name to any existing type and use the shorter alternative name instead. It can also help you to write more understandable and elegant code. This recipe is going to demonstrate how to use type aliases.

Getting ready

Let's assume we have the following two classes predefined:

```
data class Song(val title: String)
data class Artist(val name: String)
```

We are going to define a type alias for the map of `Song` type values and a generic key type–`Map<T, List<Song>>`. Next, we are going to use it to define a function that will return the most popular `Artist` instance for a given `Map<Artist, List<Song>>` object.

How to do it...

1. Declare a generic type alias for the `Map<T, List<Song>>` type:

```
typealias GrouppedSongs<T> = Map<T, List<Song>>
```

2. Implement the `getMostPopularArtist()` function using the type alias:

```
fun getMostPopularArtist(songs: GrouppedSongs<Artist>) =
    songs.toList().sortedByDescending {it.second.size
}.first().first
```

How it works...

Using the type alias, we were able to provide a custom name for the type and we could use it in `getMostPopularArtist(songs: GrouppedSongs<Artist>)` instead of `Map<Artist, List<Song>>` type, which resulted in a more meaningful declaration. We can test our implementation by invoking `getMostPopularArtist()` with sample data:

```
val songs: GrouppedSongs<Artist> =
    mapOf(
        Artist("Bob Dylan") to
            listOf(Song("Blowing In The Wind"),
                Song("To Fall in Love With You")),

        Artist("Louis Armstrong") to
            listOf(Song("What A Beautiful World"))
    )

println("${getMostPopularArtist(songs)} is the most popular")
```

As a result, we are going to get the following text printed to the console:

```
Artist(name=Bob Dylan) is most popular
```

Expressive try...catch declarations

Kotlin is advertised as an extremely expressive language. However, it's one of the characteristics of the language that is not obvious in the beginning, especially if you are used to other languages such as Java or JavaScript. In order to present the language style more clearly, in this recipe, we are going to discover how to work with the try...catch declaration in a Kotlin way, by treating it as an expression.

Getting ready

Let's consider the following Java code:

```
int value;
try {
    result = parseInt(input);
} catch (NumberFormatException e) {
} finally {
    result = 0;
}
```

It declares an int result variable. Next, it tries to parse the string value to the integer with the Integer.parseInt() function, and if it succeeds, it assigns the result to the value variable. If the parseInt() fails to parse the string, a default value of 0 is assigned to the value variable.

How to do it...

1. Invoke the parseInt() function in the try...catch declaration:

    ```
    try {
        parseInt("fdsaa")
    } catch (e: NumberFormatException) {
        0
    }
    ```

2. Assign the result of the `try...catch` declaration to the `value` variable:

```
val result = try {
    parseInt("fdsaa")
} catch (e: NumberFormatException) {
    0
}
```

How it works...

That's it. The `try...catch` declaration in Kotlin can be assigned to a variable. The reason is that it is, in fact, an expression! In our example, `try...catch` returns the result of the `parseInt()` function, and when the function throws an exception, it returns 0.

There's more...

Similarly, we can treat other language declarations as expressions. It's a common practice to assign a variable to the value returned by control flow statements, such as `if` and `when`. For example, we can use `when` as an expression in the following way:

```
val result = when(input) {
    is Int -> input
    is String -> parseInt(input)
    else -> 0
}
```

Safe type-casting

Whenever we perform type-casting, we should keep in mind that it is a potential source of exceptions. That's the reason why we should always perform type-checking using the `is` modifier or do the casting inside the `try...catch` block. However, in Kotlin, we have also a safe casting option that will not throw `ClassCastException` but will return `null` instead. In this recipe, we are going to test the safe casting in action.

How to do it...

1. Let's start by defining a function that returns a `Number` type of a random `Double` value:

```
fun getRandomNumber(): Number = Random().nextDouble() * 10
```

2. Try to cast the results of the function to different types using the safe-cast operator and print the casted values to the console:

```
println(getRandomNumber() as? Int)
println(getRandomNumber() as? Double)
println(getRandomNumber() as? String)
```

How it works...

The preceding code will not fail nor throw any exceptions. It will just return the `null` value instead. Our casting test code is going to print the following output to the console:

```
null
8.802117014997226
null
```

Using the safe `as?` casting modifier is a neat alternative to the traditional way. You can use it if you are working with nullable types, that is while working with external libraries that don't provide the null safety. However, if you can benefit from the null safety, it's best to use the standard casting operation.

Other Books You May Enjoy

If you enjoyed this book, you may be interested in these other books by Packt:

Hands-on Design Patterns with Kotlin
Alexey Soshin

ISBN: 9781788998017

- Get to grips with Kotlin principles, including its strengths and weaknesses
- Understand classical design patterns in Kotlin
- Explore functional programming using built-in features of Kotlin
- Solve real-world problems using reactive and concurrent design patterns
- Use threads and coroutines to simplify concurrent code flow
- Understand antipatterns to write clean Kotlin code, avoiding common pitfalls
- Learn about the design considerations necessary while choosing between architectures

Kotlin Programming By Example
Iyanu Adelekan

ISBN: 9781788474542

- Learn the building blocks of the Kotlin programming language
- Develop powerful RESTful microservices for Android applications
- Create reactive Android applications efficiently
- Implement an MVC architecture pattern and dependency management using Kotlin
- Centralize, transform, and stash data with Logstash
- Secure applications using Spring Security
- Deploy Kotlin microservices to AWS and Android applications to the Play Store

Leave a review - let other readers know what you think

Please share your thoughts on this book with others by leaving a review on the site that you bought it from. If you purchased the book from Amazon, please leave us an honest review on this book's Amazon page. This is vital so that other potential readers can see and use your unbiased opinion to make purchasing decisions, we can understand what our customers think about our products, and our authors can see your feedback on the title that they have worked with Packt to create. It will only take a few minutes of your time, but is valuable to other potential customers, our authors, and Packt. Thank you!

Index

www.ingramcontent.com/pod-product-compliance
Lightning Source LLC
Chambersburg PA
CBHW080638060326
40690CB00021B/4985